BEING BRITISH
What's Wrong With It?

BEING BRITISH
What's Wrong With It?

PETER WHITTLE

Biteback Publishing

First published in Great Britain in 2012 by
Biteback Publishing Ltd
Westminster Tower
3 Albert Embankment
London SE1 7SP
Copyright © Peter Whittle 2012

ISBN 978-1-84954-326-2

10 9 8 7 6 5 4 3 2 1

A CIP catalogue record for this book is available from the British Library.

Set in Filosofia and Adobe Caslon Pro
Cover design Namkwan Cho

Printed and bound in Great Britain by
CPI Group (UK) Ltd, Croydon CR0 4YY

For Halle, Raf and Zack, three young Britons

CONTENTS

THE BRITISH PATIENT

So, how do you feel? Do you think there's something wrong with being British? Or do you feel that you *should* think there's something wrong about being British? And, even if the answer to those questions is No, do you sometimes sense that there are quite a few people out there – in the paper, on the TV and radio – who certainly think there is quite definitely something wrong with it, and want to make damn sure you realise it too?

In 2012 – the year of the London Olympics and the Queen's Diamond Jubilee – it would be virtually impossible, despite all the celebrating around these national events, to answer No to all these questions. We all live in the same atmosphere, and after a couple of decades of national soul-searching, academic debates around the very meaning of what constitutes Britishness, and the occasional opportunistic intrusion from Westminster politicians, ours is a culture suffused with doubt, self-loathing and a fear for the future – if we can bring ourselves to think about the future at all. Contrary to what economists may believe, gloom and pessimism are not states of mind brought about just by financial crises – they can just as easily be the product of an acute cultural malaise. And Britain's has been about as acute as it can get.

Angry? Sad? Frustrated?

This shows itself in countless ways all around us every day, although every so often a small seemingly insignificant incident brings it home to you. While standing in a queue at a bookshop in central London recently, I overheard a conversation between the two sales assistants. Both in their early twenties, they'd obviously been discussing some social or political point (it was in the History section).

'Anyway,' said the first with a smirk by way of wrapping up, 'what has Britain ever given the world? Oh yeah, concentration camps.'

'Yeah,' agreed his colleague with a snort of derision.

My turn was next. I felt saddened for a moment, and then a sort of anger welled up inside me. But I said nothing. I glared at them a bit, although in contemporary Britain that once effective way of registering annoyance no longer really works. So I rationalised: the conversation hadn't been meant for me or the other people waiting, so I had little right to stick my oar in.

But that wasn't really the reason I kept quiet. I knew it would have appeared odd for me to take issue with what they'd been saying. I would have come across to them, and the other customers, like some sort of eccentric: what *Private Eye* used to call 'Disgusted of Tunbridge Wells'.

Besides which, these two, I'm sure, would have simply assumed those around them would agree with them, or at least wouldn't be bothered either way; they hadn't after all felt remotely inhibited about airing their views in front of us. So they would have been utterly taken aback, astonished, if I'd challenged them – if I'd started to drone on about parliamentary democracy, the industrial revolution, the rule of law, football, Shakespeare or the fact that Britain virtually shaped the world they were living in. They would have been astonished, either because they simply wouldn't have known what I was talking about, or if they did, that I should assume these were achievements to be proud of. They would have thought me some kind of ghastly reactionary nationalist, a bigot no doubt, maybe even a fascist.

But their exchange is par for the course in many circles. Self-loathing – for that is what this is – now runs through British culture to such an extent that we no longer even see it for what it is. For many, it has come to be the natural way of looking at the world. We have become used to living in a permanent state of cultural cringe which harms our society's very ability to move forward.

Being self-effacing about our achievements, reticent about our way of life, and not 'banging our own drum' when it came to national pride was once considered not just fitting, but one of the very characteristics which defined Britishness. As has been said by politicians from both parties during one of our recent spasms of argument about national identity, we do not 'do' flags in the front garden like our brash, vulgar American cousins. This is not what we're about, and goes against the very essence of Britishness. In its gentleness, the old approach was indeed quite attractive, even if it did rely on an implicit sense of imperial superiority. But if it still exists – and it does in the minds of, say, romantic old-fashioned Tories – the simple hiding of our national light under a bushel is quite different from the outright self-abnegation which in reality now characterises so many parts of our national life.

Dome and gloom

Two events in post-war Britain illustrate all too well how much things changed within the space of half a century. The Festival of Britain in 1951 was celebrated in a mood of relief for the end of the war, but also with an optimism about the future. Centred on London's South Bank, it took place in a country which still had a strong sense of itself and its achievements. The new Royal Festival Hall and the space-age symbolism of the Skylon displayed a cultural confidence which, while maybe not matching the wonders of the 1851 Great Exhibition, still proclaimed a sense of national purpose and identity. Britain might have been utterly exhausted, but it was exhausted in the knowledge that it had been victorious in a war which had brought its finest hour, during a battle which was to be viewed ever-after as a righteous one. Despite the terrible toll that the war had taken on the country and its economy, as a national celebration, the Festival could still take place in an atmosphere of remarkable social cohesion.

Furthermore, many of the people celebrating at that time would still have considered their nationality to be an intrinsic part of their very own characters. This is something which many of us, now living in the long shadows cast by the baby-boomer era, the me-generation and the counterculture of the 1960s, might find hard to understand. But the survivors of the war still took for granted the idea that somehow they were not simply their own individual inventions, but were also intrinsically formed by the nation of which they were a part. Its history was their history, its troubles their troubles. Their responses were also partly informed by a belief, taken for granted, in a set of national characteristics. I saw this in my own parents, both of whom had been teenagers at the time of the Festival. Throughout their lives – and they were both strongly individual people – they continued to explain a feeling here and an action there in collective, national terms: such and such wasn't 'the kind of thing we go in for here', or that was 'not really our cup of tea'. They knew who they were.

Now cut to half a century later. Britain again prepares to mount a popular, national celebration, this time to mark the millennium. It comes during a period when New Labour are attempting to 'rebrand' the country as a dynamic, creative powerhouse of modernity. The government, embarrassed and impatient not just with our past but with the remaining institutions that symbolise it, fatuously pronounces that we are in fact a 'young' country. It is Year Zero for Britain. So the celebration takes the shape of the super-new, super-expensive Millennium Dome. Unfortunately, because it is conceived by people who seem to have lost all confidence in Britain as well as their own personal sense of being part of it, it inevitably proves a dismal, demoralising failure.

Nobody can decide what should be in it. What it should

not be seems to preoccupy organisers far more than anything more affirmative or celebratory. Marooned outside central London, in the shadow of Canary Wharf and far away from where the crowds are actually gathering to see in the next thousand years, it is full of banal and sometimes unintentionally funny compromises. At the party held there on the eve of the new epoch, an uneasy Sovereign and a hyped-up Prime Minister link hands to sing Auld Lang Syne with all the awkwardness of a first date. Unlike the 1951 festival, or even more so the 1851 Great Exhibition, the Dome manages, with its 'zones' and supposedly visitor-friendly attractions, to both patronise and condescend in its attempts to be accessible and popular. As a result, the people stay away in their millions. In its afterlife, and roughly a billion pounds later, the Dome manages finally to find fame as a popular – if windswept – venue for rock gigs.

What happened during those fifty years? When exactly did we become so sheepish, so tentative, so inhibited? When did British culture change from one which had a basic pride in itself, a pride which could be taken for granted, into one in which a seemingly endless apology, even an outright repudiation of everything about ourselves and our story, was dominant? And why?

The aim of this book is to attempt to answer these vital questions. In the following chapters, we will explore the ways in which we got to where we are now, and how we ended up in what, in modern parlance, might be called a Bad Place. But we will not just be backward-looking; it is not the intention of this exercise to simply offer up a lament. We will examine the options and in doing so, try to come to a prognosis. Is the British patient on life support, as the more pessimistic amongst us believe? Has it lost all belief in itself? Is it, moreover, on some kind of suicide mission, happy to let itself waste away?

Or is it simply that for too long the wrong people have been in charge of its wellbeing? Is there underneath it all a basically strong constitution which, even if glimpsed from time to time, remains largely hidden from day to day? And if it wants to survive and flourish in the future, what are the best courses of action it can take?

Should we, indeed, be cautiously optimistic?

A self-harming nation

The popular feeling that Britain seems determined to rubbish itself is not the result of some kind of mass hallucination. There has certainly been a sustained cultural onslaught over the past forty years, one which has left Britain not just at sea about its very identity, but at a loss as to its own history, its 'back story' as screenwriters call it. Its institutions have been either trashed or called into question, its habits and traditions traduced. None of this has been done, however, via the ballot box, or as the result of popular demand from the grassroots.

Britain's post-war economic history, its slow withdrawal from first-class status as a world power, and the remarkably rapid dismantling of its former Empire would combine to have a huge effect on national confidence. Britain, of which it was famously said in the 1950s, had 'lost an empire and has yet to find a role'. But this in itself does need lead inevitably and naturally to the self-loathing and self-abnegation which dominates our culture now. It is perfectly possible to be in diminished circumstances, and yet still have pride, still be comfortable in one's own skin, still know, in essence, who one is.

Similarly the acts and omissions of decades of politicians might cause one to despair, and even feel shame at policies carried out in the country's name. But being ashamed of one's government is quite distinct from being ashamed of one's country, and shouldn't be confused. Unless, of course, one actively wants to be ashamed of one's country – in which case, governments will provide ample opportunities.

Rather, it is those who set the tone of our national life, those who shape the cultural landscape, who have had a powerful hand in making the country unrecognisable to those who were born and formed here, and unknowable to those who come here now. They have done a wonderful job of it.

When one starts talking variously about the metropolitan liberal elite, the political/media class, the chattering classes and so forth, it's not uncommon for a glazed, bored look to come into the eyes of others. The terms seem nebulous and abstract. But as we shall see later the importance of what would once have been called 'the great and the good' when it comes to Britain's self-image cannot be underestimated. It largely sets the agenda.

There is a 'trickle-down' effect here. The elite's worldview determines what is considered acceptable and what is undesirable. It sets the terms of debate under which everybody else has to operate. This is not to say that there is anything sinister going on here; this is not some kind of weird conspiracy.

It is simply to state that there tends to be a remarkable convergence of beliefs and views amongst this group. And for anybody who questions its existence the recent referendum on whether Britain should adopt the AV system for future elections provided fascinating evidence. The result, which provided a massive win for the No campaign, also showed that of just ten areas to return a 'Yes' were Islington and Camden in London as well as Oxford, Cambridge and central Edinburgh. Here for all to see were the habitats of the metropolitan liberal elites, the members of the self-styled 'progressive alliance'.

An anorexic nation

If one of the causes of anorexia is a chronic lack of self-esteem, or possibly a desire to make oneself disappear altogether, then there is a case for saying that Britain has become an anorexic country. The symptoms of this condition are all around us. One can look around at random and up they will pop.

So, for example: a perusal of the broadsheet 'quality' press and its resident commentators at any one time will reveal a steady flow of casually derogatory and snobbish remarks and observations about Britain and the British, ranging from their past historical achievements down to their eating habits.

On television, one can watch a documentary which aims to show that there is nothing intrinsically British about anybody living in these islands, that we are just a mishmash, and that we are not who we might think we are. Switch channels, and one can hear a liberal former newspaper editor on a programme supposedly celebrating Britishness, citing, in a model of negative reasoning, our acceptance of other cultures as the chief reason she is proud to be British.

Or take the world of the arts: a long-dead playwright, once celebrated for his depiction of innately British characters and subject matter, undergoes a mild, somewhat knowing critical reappraisal only after decades of being reviled and mocked for the very same thing. This is reflected in many ordinary, social conversations, where reticence, restraint, pragmatism, a belief that our institutions were probably the best in an imperfect world, a wariness of new-fangled ideologies – things that once went towards defining British culture – can now only be referred to ironically, with a set of silent quote marks around them. One is encouraged to find them funny at best, completely destructive at worst. Or simply mythical: George Orwell might have written of the essential gentleness of our national character and hence culture but now it appears that we want to disown that gentleness – indeed, we are all too ready to be convinced that it never really existed.

Or turn to the political sphere, if you can bear to: a front-bench Labour politician proclaims that Britain is only the country it is because of immigration (and therefore without it we would be nothing; the wince-inducing insult in the comment appeared lost on her). While on a trip to Pakistan, the Prime Minister ensures that the cult of political apology for our past sins as a nation, whether real or imagined, remains a feature of modern diplomacy. A Chancellor of the Exchequer, who will one day bleat about the need for a national 'conversation' on British identity, presides over the quiet removal of Britannia from the coinage.

And finally: official statistics reveal that a record number of people are leaving Britain, while a new survey confirms that many more would join them if they could afford it.

To say that examples such as these have a drip-drip effect on national morale must surely be an understatement. When taken as a whole, they are evidence of a cultural crisis which goes way beyond healthy self-analysis.

A nation with severe memory loss

It came as a shock to many recently when a survey of young people found that an alarmingly high number of them thought Winston Churchill was a fictional character. Many of those who are involved with the training and hiring of young people would be far less surprised.

A person who doesn't know his own past has no idea who he is, and certainly has no sense of how to deal with whatever the future might throw at him. So it is with a country. As the American philosopher George Santayana said, 'A country without a memory is a country of madmen.'

The jettisoning of meaningful chronological history in our educational system has resulted in whole generations who have little idea of the country in which they live, its history and traditions, let alone what made it great. The educational establishment has been more obsessed with social engineering, with matters of class, gender and race, than in teaching our national story. But it goes further than this: the darker episodes in our history have been highlighted to such an extent that it has instilled a sense of shame.

The framework that national self-knowledge once provided

has therefore been dismantled. Cut adrift from its moorings in this way, our society – or large parts of it – has instead taken refuge in the superficial and the trashy. One doesn't have to be some kind of religious fundamentalist to despair of the tone and preoccupations of much of modern British life. Vacant, hugely sentimental and yet aggressive, it sometimes seems to be dominated by self-absorption and impatience. This, along with its apparent obsession with cheap and tawdry celebrity, feels frankly alien to those who might remember times being different not so long ago. It sometimes seems that there is no link to be found, no organic evolution, between the Britain of now and the Britain of just a few decades ago.

Self-harming, anorexic, amnesiac. Anything else?

It might appear that I am piling on the agony here. There are those who might say that in doing so, I am behaving in a uniquely British way. We have always complained about the country going to the dogs, they would say; and they'd be right on that: we always have. But for the reasons I have described, I believe our current malaise is of quite a different order. And judging by the number of anxious, bewildered and quietly angry people one comes across on a daily basis, both young and old, I am far from being alone.

Alongside the general cultural drift I've referred to already there have been other, huge factors in the post-war era which have had a direct bearing on British identity and self-image. The first and unquestionably the most important has been the doctrine of multiculturalism. Now slowly being disowned by European countries including this one, it has nevertheless had a profound social and cultural impact. Somewhat late in the day, its all-pervading influence is being judged to have been baleful.

Many of the supporters of multiculturalism – which has for years been enshrined as an article of faith, followed to the word by those liberal elites – were no doubt naive but well-intentioned believers in the brotherhood of man, people who saw it as just an advanced form of cultural good manners. But there were certainly, too, those who saw in it a highly effective weapon with which to attack a mainstream culture which, for a myriad of reasons, they despised.

Multiculturalism might well have failed. What has been very successful over the past two decades, however, is the attempt to portray any concerns about it, or about the historically unprecedented levels of immigration into Britain, variously as racist, bigoted or xenophobic. Despite this being the topic of greatest importance so far as millions of people are concerned, it is hardly surprising that, with the torrent of abuse they feel they would suffer, many Britons are now tentative about voicing even the mildest of qualms. Many have decided, understandably, that it's best to simply keep their mouths shut.

Clowns to the left of us, jokers to the right

There are two other issues of great importance so far as Britain and Britishness is concerned, but which if raised could be guaranteed, until recently at least, to clear any room: Europe and devolution. Both of these have been treated by the general public as peripheral topics of interest chiefly to

Westminster politicians and politics junkies, and of little importance in their everyday lives. That has changed quite remarkably in the past few years, as more and more people have woken up to the fact that the UK seems to be caught in some kind of pincer movement, between those who want it to break up from the inside, and those who want it to be fully submerged into something bigger on the outside.

The dislike and fear of nationalism to which we referred earlier, and the belief that the single nation was something which was essentially out of date, were always motivating forces behind support for the EU. As we'll see later, anybody who demurred from this view tended to be written off as hopelessly old-fashioned and backward-looking. More than that – our old friend xenophobia was again pressed into action and used as an accusation to silence all opposition. But the inconvenient fact remained that, economics aside, most Britons remained stubbornly unimpressed with the whole idea. Even now, Britain tends not to think of itself as European in the way mainland continental countries might. The EU's own surveys have consistently shown that British faith or even interest in the European 'project' is the lowest of all the member countries (bar Latvia). And with the current and ongoing crisis over the euro, opposition to the EU can no longer be so easily written off as the ravings of a gang of Little Englanders.

Given this, it's paradoxical that such hostility to nasty, inward-looking, possibly bellicose nationalism often went hand-in-hand with an unquestioning support for the Scottish and Welsh variety. In other words, certain sorts of nationalism were politically perfectly acceptable to those on the liberal left – largely because it struck right at the heart of the idea of Britain. Now, in the aftermath of devolution, and with the prospect of a referendum on full Scottish independence, we're faced with the very real possibility that the United Kingdom as we've known it will cease to exist.

Multiculturalism, Europe, Scottish and Welsh devolution – any one of these issues, taken alone, would have implications for the whole idea of what it means to be British. Put together they constitute a triple whammy. And when you add into the mix the self-hatred, the collapse in confidence and the never-ending carping, the only surprise is not why many of us question just what's so wrong with being British, but why more of us don't.

Reasons to be cheerful

That Britain is a remarkable country there is no doubt. It seems, however, to have forgotten this. It badly needs to be reminded.

But is it a lost cause? Has the moment come when the country might wither away through the sheer neglect and indifference of those who inhabit its increasingly bulging borders? Do enough people care about being British?

Whatever the answer to that turns out to be, and we shall explore it in greater detail further on, it would be foolish to deny that many have come to the conclusion that there is little point in caring about a country that seems not to care about itself anymore. Some indeed go further than this, and start to actively hate a place they were once fond of, simply because they perceive it (or more likely, the government) to be weak, or cowardly, or on yet another self-destructive course. It's to be hoped that such people can, and should, be won round again.

I remember having similarly ambivalent feelings myself a couple of years ago, when a group of British sailors were taken captive by the Iranians. The acute embarrassment one felt was not so much due to the incident itself as to the subsequent behaviour of the hostages and the way this must have played out to an international audience. Traumatised and simpering, complaining of having their iPods taken, giving anguished interviews to the media on their return – the comportment of these serviceman and women was mortifying to witness. Such moments as these really do give one pause: was I simply holding on to an idea of Britain and its people which no longer corresponded in any shape or form to the reality? Was I kidding myself?

Keeping faith

All it takes to restore my faith on occasions such as this is to find out quite how many people feel exactly the same way. For others though it might take a lot more. How many times have you seen a resigned shrug of the shoulders followed by the question, 'But what *does* British mean these days?' People can't be blamed for asking it, for although some might be parroting lines from the latest media discussion on the subject, others will be asking out of a genuine sense of bemusement and loss. And this will be followed by other questions, sometimes asked angrily, sometimes in sadness, sometimes in frustration:

'Why do I feel that I should keep quiet about being proud to be British?' or 'What is it that we should be ashamed of, and apologise for?' and 'Why am I frightened of being called an extremist if I want to celebrate being British?'

As we shall see further on, patriotism, national pride – call it what you like – has shown a remarkable capacity for survival in Britain, against what might seem to have been insuperable odds, and certainly in the face of active discouragement. And it is also clear that a coming together of the nation can still happen. It certainly tends to take many by surprise, and the disapproving generally hold their noses until the parade passes by. We saw it with the Falklands War back in 1982, and the Queen's Golden Jubilee twenty years later.

But what are its chances in the future? As I said earlier, the aim of this book is not to celebrate something that has passed, not to provide a memorial or an elegy. But if we are to be constructive, and offer suggestions as to how a sense of national identity can be sustained and indeed promoted, we will have to consider whether the old ways of doing things are really adequate in the twenty-first century. We will have to establish whether the rules of the game have changed so drastically in the modern, globalised world that a totally new approach is needed – one which might not immediately appeal to those who grew up in a different, gentler time. It might become clear that a much more proactive, less passive attitude is needed if Britain is to successfully maintain any real sense of what it is, was, and could be in the future.

CHAPTER ONE

VETOES, RIOTS AND ROYALS

Britain had an eventful year in 2011. A royal wedding in the spring, a spate of urban rioting in the summer which seemed to come out of nowhere, and a mounting crisis in the EU which culminated at the end of the year in the use of a veto by the British Prime Minister, leaving the UK apparently alone and unloved by the other twenty-six member states. It was a good year, for our purposes, to take stock, for all of these events held a mirror up to the state of Britain and told us something about its sense of itself. The messages were distinctly mixed.

Like 1981 all over again?

In some respects 2011 felt like a rerun of thirty years earlier. There were some remarkable similarities with that equally eventful year: as before, people dusted off bunting and cheered a new royal couple, there were again calls in the press for rubber bullets to be used on rampaging looters, and the average man in the street still tried to get his head around the precise difference between a European treaty and a simple agreement (and then quickly gave up). There were demonstrations about the 'swingeing' cuts in public spending, there was a (nominally) Conservative government in control (albeit as the senior partner in a coalition), and on TV there was a nostalgic drama about aristocratic country-house life which was proving to be an unexpected hit with viewers.

But although the popularity of *Downton Abbey* might convince the casual observer that Britain's tastes, preoccupations and sense of itself had remained reassuringly the same as when viewers had switched on to *Brideshead Revisited* all those years ago, in many fundamental respects Britain had changed quite drastically. In 1981 pubs still enjoyed their place at the centre of social life up and down the country. PC meant police constable, not political correctness. People laughed at the same jokes told by the same comedians, and they would have assumed that reality television meant documentaries. Devolution was just a twinkle in Alex Salmond's eye. Suicide bombing was quite literally alien, something that happened in the far-off Middle East. When England played an international game, crowds waved the Union flag. People were not called upon to state their ethnicity on local government forms. They still queued. Nobody talked much about British Identity.

But the early 1980s are interesting to look at for another reason. For a brief period, there was a resurgence, a kind of Indian summer, of a particular sort of traditional Britishness, which could be seen not just in the events of the time but in the culture that surrounded them. After years of egalitarian drabness, and a whole decade in which the country appeared to be in inexorable decline, the early 1980s saw what might appear, looking back, to be a sort of last hurrah, a purple blast, of a Britishness which was nostalgic, traditionally hierarchical, and had a popular awareness of its recently departed imperial past.

The Empire strikes back

Undoubtedly the centrepiece of this mini-era was provided by the Falklands War. It came as a surprise to most people not only to see that Britain still had the wherewithal to mount an effective military challenge to an act of overseas aggression (albeit a minor one), but that it still had sufficient will to do so, and to act on that will without prevarication. The war was supported by the public, as was seen by the extraordinary crowds which turned out to greet the return of the Task Force. Thousands came to wave flags and cheer; it was the biggest display of patriotism not linked either to a sporting event or royal occasion that the country had seen since the end of the Second World War, and certainly there has been nothing like it since.

The crowds were good-humoured and there was nothing aggressively nationalistic about their motives. This, however, did not stop the carping and tut-tutting of the chattering, leftish elites who found it all too ghastly and jingoistic for words, and who then proceeded to obsess about the sinking of the Argentinean ship the *Belgrano*. Similarly, the liberal sentiments expressed by the Archbishop of Canterbury at the Memorial Service at St Paul's, during which he coupled both

Argentinean and British troops together in remembrance, were predictable enough, although this didn't stop Prime Minister Margaret Thatcher from reportedly 'spitting blood' with anger over it.

The fact remained that the war had happened, and had been successful, and had been seen as a wholly British thing, proof that we could still do it, if pushed. It had been conducted by a Prime Minister who talked utterly unashamedly of her pride in being British, who had made it her mission to ensure that the country did not accept that its decline was inevitable and irreversible. Such bullishness made her an object of scorn amongst those who, discerning echoes of Empire and insufficient defeatism in her exhortation to the country to congratulate its armed forces ('Just rejoice at that news!'), found such sentiments distasteful. Not that she cared; far more importantly, it had had the effect of galvanising many, many more, who had increasingly felt that their once great country could no longer be relied upon to walk unaided.

Lords, ladies and highwaymen

That we could also still mount world-class ceremonial occasions had been shown the year before, when Charles married Diana in what was to be globally the most viewed royal event up to that point. Popular celebration in the summer of 1981 exceeded that which had accompanied the wedding even of the Queen during the gloom of the post-war period, despite taking place against a background of urban rioting. There were the Labour activists who ostentatiously set sail for France to get away from it all, and the odd anti-wedding 'festival', but overwhelmingly the country was behind it, bedecking itself in red, white and blue and almost high with the apparently perfect fairy-tale aspect of the whole thing.

And it was, compared to the wedding of 2011, unapologetically aristocratic. Indeed after the nihilism of punk rock, and the grinding drabness of much of the 1970s, Britain in the early 1980s seemed to be going through some kind of resurgence of traditionalism of a very particular kind. At the cinema, *Chariots of Fire*, a tale of two hearty gentlemen runners competing at the 1924 Olympics, was one of the year's biggest hits, going on to win Oscars and prompting its screenwriter Colin Welland to (somewhat prematurely) declare 'The British are Coming!' On TV we had not only *Brideshead* and its loving, almost voyeuristic portrayal of an ancient aristocratic family, but the spectacular drama series *The Jewel in the Crown*, about the British in India before the end of an Empire on which the sun was never meant to set. One of the year's most popular books was the only slightly tongue-in-cheek *The Official Sloane Ranger Handbook*, a guide to the habits and habitats of the British upper classes, which was laughed at by some and treated as a bible of aspiration by many more. The social season, of balls, Ascot and Henley, which had long before been pronounced moribund, enjoyed a sudden revival. And in the charts, a particularly British kind of pop reigned: the New Romantics, led by Adam and his Ants, sang about highwaymen and ostentatiously displayed a singularly British love of camp fancy dress.

Of course it was perfectly possible to hate all of this and yet still have a pride in being British. It would be quite wrong to immediately link patriotism with nostalgia, a love of royal ceremonial and a disproportionate level of interest in aristocratic tastes. A strong sense of national identity need not be allied to these things; it can be born out of completely different traditions, and indeed has been in Britain. There was, too, still a level of deference in British society then which it was perfectly possible to deplore on political grounds without it signifying a general dislike of the nation. But the early 1980s remain fascinating because, after the countercultural upheaval of the sixties, its blind belief in youth, and its revolutionary questioning of all traditional values and institutions, followed by the trade-union dominated politics of the 1970s, it was a time when, all of a sudden, it seemed that the old Britain – or an aspect of it at least – was back and riding high in the saddle. It was an epoch which was to prove very brief, failing to outlast the arrival of the yuppie, Big Bang, Loadsamoney and the rest of the iconography more usually associated with the Thatcher era. It was perhaps the last stand of a culture that was undergoing a huge transformation: an unconscious counter-counter-revolution.

Saying no

By 2011, the early 1980s felt as remote as the Festival of Britain. When at the end of the year Prime Minister David Cameron exercised Britain's veto at one of the interminable conferences called to make sense of the Eurozone crisis, it was probably the first time since the Falklands War that Britain had said No to a set of foreign demands. Nearly thirty years had passed and most British people had got used to the country trimming its sails here, rolling with the punches there, not really saying boo to a goose. It might account for the genuine spring in the step that so many – and not just Eurosceptics – felt on hearing the news. Britain appeared alone, as the other members queued to sign up – perhaps the first time in history, it was pointed out at the time, that rats elected to join a sinking ship.

Hard-line opponents of Britain's membership of the EU maintained of course that in reality Cameron had done no such thing, that the veto was meaningless (a view they reiterated some months later, when Cameron's resolve appeared to weaken). Others claimed that in refusing to accept a new set of rules that would have affected Britain's financial sector and the special position held by the City in the economy, the Prime Minister was simply helping his banker friends. But in some ways this was to miss the point; it was the symbolism that mattered. And sure enough, opinion polls showed that around 55 per cent of those asked approved of his action. It was not so much that they understood the labyrinthine workings of the EU, neither did it mean they loved Cameron any the more; rather, they liked the fact that the country's leader had been seen to stand up for its interests in the face of opposition.

The euro crisis, and the unravelling of the European project which came with it and continued to intensify, caused a media-wide searching of the soul about Britain's place in Europe. An opinion poll in the *Sunday Times* found that 54 per cent of those asked said they believed that the main political parties had tried to suppress debate about Britain's membership. A full 70 per cent believed that the country should try to renegotiate its treaties with Europe. Most strikingly, 54 per cent thought that Britain should leave the EU altogether, a figure which was in line with other surveys showing the 50 per cent barrier being broken for the first time.

In other words, being sceptical about Europe, or indeed, believing that Britain should go the whole way and call it a day were, in 2011, becoming mainstream views. This was a remarkable change. Traditionally the public's general reaction towards the whole subject had been one of either bored, vague hostility or agitated indifference. Certainly they had never really taken to the idea of a pan-European identity: this resistance was echoed in the EU's own regular surveys, which found that identification as 'European' was the lowest in Britain of all of the members states (who can forget that famous headline 'Fog in channel: Continent cut off'?) Trust in the EU's institutions was similarly lowest in Britain. Not that most British people had been against the idea of a single market: when in 1975 they thought they were voting in a referendum for what was then known as the EEC, or Common Market, they had returned a clear Yes. But by 2011, it had become quite clear to even those least interested in the topic that they had not been told the whole story.

Swivel-eyed loony toons

What also became clear was that those who had warned against the dangers of a common currency, or had had deeper qualms about the general loss of British sovereignty, had been treated appallingly. Their arguments had been dismissed by the Europhile governing class who did their best to shut them up by insulting them as xenophobes, Little Englanders and head-in-the-sand reactionaries. When the journalist Rod Liddle, then editor of Radio 4's *Today* programme, suggested to the executive in charge of the BBC's political impartiality that maybe there should be more even airtime given to sceptics, the answer came back: 'Ron, the thing you have to understand is that these people are mad. They are mad.'

'The whole ethos of the BBC and all of the staff was that Eurosceptics were xenophobes and Little Englanders and there was the end of it,' Liddle has since said. 'The euro would come up at a meeting and everybody would just burst out laughing about the Eurosceptics. Beyond all doubt the BBC was institutionally in favour of the single currency. That was the BBC position – of that there is no doubt at all.'

There it was: these swivel-eyed reactionaries were on the wrong side of history, and should be ignored in the hope that eventually they'd wither and die. They were, in essence, considered to be the wrong type of British people – the kind who clung obstinately onto an idea of a nation and its currency, and didn't believe that the future lay in top-down superstates.

Not that the euro crisis brought forth many *meae culpae* from the powerful and vocal supporters of Europe and the euro. A few prominent commentators, such as Sir Max Hastings and *The Times* columnist Matthew Parris, wrote articles recanting on their previous full-throated support. The journalist Peter Oborne published a pamphlet, *Guilty Men*, which called to account those respected institutions – including the *Financial*

Times and the BBC that had made the case for Britain's membership of the euro while at the same time denigrating those opposed to it, often in highly personal terms. Over the past decade the language used by the pro-euro gang had frequently gone way beyond the normal boundaries of public discourse. 'We could stop listening to the assorted maniacs, buffoons, empire-nostalgists, colonial press tycoons, Save the Groat anoraks and Yorkshire separatists of the Europhobe movement, and prepare for our earliest feasible entry into the euro,' David Aaronovitch had written in *The Independent* in 2001, which, while capturing the flavour of the pro-euro argument, was revealing in the utter contempt it displayed for those who were, eventually, to be proved right.

As the euro crisis of 2011 wore on with seemingly no end in sight, there was an embarrassed, irritated silence from most of its erstwhile cheerleaders. In the end this didn't matter much; they knew who they were, and that they'd miscalculated badly. It was perhaps best to keep quiet. But what did all of this tell us about the state of Britishness? What was it that had brought forth such bile?

The wrong type of British

Much of it was surely about being in the right gang in the playground. Nobody wants to be the nerd or the oddball, and witnessing the onslaught endured by the Eurosceptics would surely be enough to have put off any possible waverers. In this case, the nerds and the oddballs were those who the smarter metropolitan types decided, with their limited imaginations, were throwbacks: white, middle-class, old-fashioned, suburban, members of rotary clubs perhaps, *Daily Mail* readers almost certainly. They were probably small-minded patriots, with prejudices instead of opinions. One wouldn't want to be associated with *them*.

So much of the Europhiles' disdain was born partly of a kind of snobbery, partly of something as superficial as style. It echoed a similar hostility which had been felt towards Ulster Unionists: they were mostly men, they wore suits, they weren't heavily into irony, and fads and trends seemed to pass them by. These things would condemn them in fashionable, liberal, politically correct eyes just as much as their strongly held political convictions. Of course these were all horrendous stereotypes: many Eurosceptics were young, many were women, certainly not all of them were white. But it suited their tormentors to paint them as such. They were types not wanted in modern, dynamic, young, diverse Britain.

The more important point, however, is that they had committed one of the cardinal modern sins: they had gone against one of the decided political orthodoxies of our time. Like climate change, the science so far as the EU was concerned was 'settled', and woe betide anybody who questioned it. Europe was obviously a force for good, and those who thought otherwise were either mad or bad.

The EU was just one of a set of topics on which, in modern Britain, there was a 'correct' view. It is hard to think of an era in which public discussion has been more prescribed, when the pressure to confirm to a set of political or social values has been so great. Immigration and multiculturalism, as we shall see later, was another such area, as was environmentalism; and alongside this went a whole host of social issues on which, for so long, there had also been an 'acceptable' approach to take – crime, education and welfare, for example. The result was a widening gap between the rulers and the ruled.

Very well then, alone?

But the events of 2011 meant that not only was one of these shibboleths crumbling, but that the scepticism which had for so long been caricatured and shunned was stepping out of the shadows and becoming completely respectable. With it came the realisation that those nasty xenophobes might actually have been principled, thoughtful individuals with Britain's interests uppermost in their minds. People remarked on how quickly, ultimately, this change occurred; quite a few of them felt relieved.

And there was this too: for decades the British had been told by those who governed them that, frankly, they were nothing without the EU. The country, they were informed, would be adrift, a mere afterthought, of no consequence whatsoever. It would have no place to go in the modern world. This line of argument proved to be very effective in winning over the more recalcitrant. Many people who, while not actively hostile to the EU, had had instinctive qualms about it as a political project, were convinced enough to put their reservations aside. The effect of all this was to add to the sense that being British now had a knocked-down value, that on its own Britain was pretty worthless. It's depressing that so many were ready to believe it, but then if it is your own rulers who are telling you this, you could be forgiven for, as it were, internalising the message.

But as 2011 came to an end and things continued to crumble in Euroland, cautious reassessment of the received wisdom became not just a pleasure for those who'd always had their doubts, but an intellectual duty for all but the most bigoted Europhiles. So we might be on our own. So what? As one wit put it, we would be isolated in the way that a lone man waving off the *Titanic* from the dock is isolated.

Brokeback Britain

If the fall-out from the euro crisis had left many feeling not quite so beleaguered about the country's prospects, or indeed about being British, and had given many a reason to be cheerful, then the riots that had sprung up in the cities in the summer of 2011 intensified the fears many had for what was happening nearer to home.

The fuse for the worst civil disturbances seen since the early 1980s was lit, on the face of it, by the police shooting of gang member Mark Duggan in Tottenham in north London. But the violence quickly took on a life of its own, and the rapidity with which it spread across the capital, virtually unopposed by the police, took everybody by surprise. Lulled into complacency by the official line of London being a massive, post-national city state success, people were horrified and incredulous at the sight of department stores engulfed in flames and rampant, unrestrained feral looting. The trouble spread to other towns and cities, and then stopped almost as quickly as it arose. The effect was like a violent jolt.

As shopkeepers started to pick through the charred remnants of their livelihoods and volunteers swept away the shattered glass, the spectre of what had become known as 'Broken Britain' loomed over the discussion about exactly what had happened and why. In the media, with wearying predictability, a long succession of 'youth workers' and 'community leaders' began to wail and gnash about unemployment, lack of opportunity, and, in a couple of ridiculous instances, even poverty-induced hunger. It was the same old lame excuse-making, but with one difference: few people were buying it this time.

The existence of 24-hour news, mobile phones, Twitter, Facebook and, not least, ubiquitous security cameras, had brought all of it much nearer than ever before – we could see the animalistic behaviour and the triumphant posturing up close for ourselves. We could hear clearly the sheer glee, the delight in destruction that characterised so much of it. The victory laps on social media sites and the endless use of instantaneous messaging meant that the rioters hanged themselves with their own deeds and words.

The picture of moral and social anarchy was simply undeniable, and all but the most dogmatic of the usual apologists for such disturbances were at a loss – for once – for words. Even so, the narrative of London as an all-singing all-dancing melting pot of vibrant, swinging diversity had to be quickly reinstated, and there was much talk of how the riots had brought out the best in Londoners, who were coming out and standing firm etc. The Blitz spirit was played up.

But in many ways the disturbances dangerously exposed the extent of fragmentation in the capital, and indeed the country. The media coverage tended to portray the different communities readying themselves to protect life and limb as evidence of people coming together. But the picture one was ultimately left with was of quite separate blocks of people operating above a low buzz of tension. Sikhs were approvingly shown locking arms to protect their temple and community from looters, and the Turks of Dalston similarly won praise for defending their patch. The broom-wielding cleaner-uppers who appeared in the aftermath were largely white. The groups of mostly working-class white men who came out in force in lower middle-class suburbs, predictably, alarmed the liberal media, which has a tendency to smell incipient fascism whenever a group of young white men assemble. In Birmingham, three Asian men were killed in a hit-and-run by a car driven by a black man, an incident which briefly highlighted tensions between those two groups.

... or Brokeback England?

That all ethnicities took part in the riots was without doubt, although in London at least, the high proportion of young black rioters tended to be played down. But despite the fact that multiculturalism in Britain had for some time been talked of as a dismal failure, it was still deemed imperative by many in the media to emphasise it was in no way responsible for the events of August 2011.

It was impossible not to note, however, that the riots were confined to England, and mostly urban areas at that. Scotland and Wales, which have seen less of the dislocation wrought by mass immigration, and where the doctrine of multiculturalism has remained therefore largely theoretical, were unaffected. This is not to say that different ethnicities necessarily have a greater propensity to riot, but rather that the fragmentation and breakdown in a sense of community which are brought on by large-scale mass immigration certainly contribute to an environment in which people have little connection to the place around them, and in which rioting and the like are more likely to happen.

The riots were the product not so much of a strong, confident culture but, it seemed, of a very fragile one. Did they unite Britain at all? Certainly there was a sense, directly afterwards, that people were treating each other with a little more consideration in small, everyday ways. There was also the sense that this had been something which had been done to us, not by us. But these feelings did not last. We were, ultimately, left with the knowledge that there was a large section of us who had no sense of communal feeling, whether it be local or national. There were serious ruptures in the social infrastructure which, while conveniently out of sight much of the time, had suddenly made themselves terribly visible.

What Britain does best

The pictures that flashed around the world of burning buildings could not have been in greater contrast to those which had held a fair amount of it enthralled only a few months earlier. Prince William's marriage to Catherine Middleton in April had provided the world with the kind of spectacle which it had traditionally expected from Britain, but which it was no longer completely sure it could expect. The years since 1981's royal wedding had, after all, been tough for the monarchy. And the world had gathered that Britain had changed. Americans in particular had become gradually aware that the country they'd always admired for producing fastidious, immaculately tasteful costume dramas they could lap up on their own televisions no longer seemed that fastidious or immaculately tasteful, and could easily out-trash them when it came to TV. Would they still tune in?

In the event it worked, and worked flawlessly. All the traditional elements – carriage processions, gleaming breastplates, balcony appearances – remained in place, but the ambiance was remarkably fresh, even modern. There was not a single false or jarring note. Unlike at the wedding of thirty years earlier, the congregation consisted of a wider cross section of contemporary Britain – including a fair share of celebrity faces. The lesser royals travelled in minibuses, and at the end of the day the newlyweds drove themselves off in a small sports-car festooned with balloons. These stylistic innovations did not, however, have an apologetic air about them. Indeed from start to finish, the royal wedding felt happily and confidently British.

There was an international audience of over two billion – which also ensured as a nice by-product that Britain's future Head of State would be familiar in every part of the globe. In Britain, 25 million watched on television, which, in an era when 6 million viewers is enough to make a hit, made it one of the biggest TV audiences in years. About a million more lined the route, and provided the world's cameras with extraordinary scenes as they cheered the couple on the Palace balcony. Later in the year, over 600,000 queued to see the

bride's dress displayed at the Palace. There were 5,000 offi-
cially registered local street party celebrations, although the
gatherings held in pubs, gardens and private homes made
the final total far higher.

Did the wedding provide an opportunity, even fleeting, to
feel good about being British? Yes, in that for a few days the
country appeared happy, and was brought together, although
the level of interest certainly varied throughout the UK; in
Scotland there was noticeably less enthusiasm, just as there
had been less celebration at the time of the Queen's Golden
Jubilee in 2002. The fact remained, however, that outside
sporting events, royal occasions such as the wedding continued to provide one of the few opportunities for Britain to
express itself in a national, collective way.

Some undoubtedly celebrated with a measure of irony and
knowingness. But in the main, the support for the event was
sincere. There was no shame at being seen to wave a Union
Jack, or at being moved by the singing of 'Jerusalem' in
Westminster Abbey. It was gratifying to see the inspired reaction of passers-by as they took pictures on their phones of the
magnificent display of Union flags that bedecked the whole
of London's Regent Street. Furthermore, there was some
satisfaction to be had in seeing the world's media descend on
the capital and make Britain the focus of the world's attention, and in a positive light at that.

Were things looking up?

The public reactions to the wedding, the riots and the euro
crisis were all in their different ways interesting to those

attempting to gauge how Britain felt about itself. If one were to glimpse the country from afar in 2011, then it might well seem that, actually, Britain had a strong idea of what it was, that it was still a country patriotic enough to celebrate along with its royal family, that it closed ranks, at least for a while, in the face of appalling riots, and that its basic sense of individualism had reasserted itself in its growing hostility to what had been seen to be the natural and inevitable growth of European federalism.

But this was of course certainly far from being the whole story. On a day-to-day level, this was not, as the visiting US-based journalist Andrew Sullivan had claimed (with unfortunate timing, just before the riots), a country relaxed and happy in its own skin. If it were, then why would one hear so many conversations about how Britain seemed finished? Why would people strike an apologetic, careful tone before telling you that they were proud of being British but felt guilty for saying so? Or that they were proud of being English, but feared they would be branded *racist* for saying so?

And why would one be struck by the anger and frustration of complete strangers, emotions which took little time to come to the surface during ordinary everyday exchanges? Why would there seem to be such a widespread feeling that it was simply no longer acceptable to say what you believed about national issues? And why did I come across so many people in 2011 who were seriously considering emigrating?

The ongoing financial crisis certainly makes people feel insecure and pessimistic. But the fear that it engenders, while being very real, is not what is behind the feelings and questions I've just mentioned. It is dismay of a different sort – one, I believe, which comes from a society which has had its sense of itself effectively hollowed out. To misquote Bill Clinton, it is not the economy, stupid. It is the cultural state we're in.

CHAPTER TWO

THEM AND US

N ot everybody felt inclined to raise a glass to William and Kate in 2011. Not out of some personal spite, but rather from an instinctive antipathy to such displays of national fervour, especially when it related to all things monarchical. Of course, one can feel a strong sense of national identity and pride without necessarily being a monarchist. Britain has a strong tradition of grassroots radicalism; it was cutting off the heads of kings long before anybody else had thought of it. But the types who tended to be sniffy about the royal wedding were often to be found amongst the higher reaches of national life, in the cultural and academic worlds, the political class, the movers and shakers of the media world, the intelligentsia. And they came from a much more modern tradition.

George Orwell said that the intellectuals of this country were unique in that they were characterised by a dislike of their own nationality. They 'would rather steal from a poor-box,' he wrote, 'than stand for God Save the King.' The so-called intelligentsia have always had a distaste not just for Britain and Britishness, but a dislike of the very idea of 'the nation', which was seen as the font of all that was evil in the world, such as nationalism and war. Alongside this they often had a horror of the 'crowd', the masses, as well as an overdeveloped preference for and fascination with other cultures.

But most importantly, they have in the past century also always enjoyed an influence and an access to policy-making and opinion-forming which is hugely disproportionate to their numbers. From Virginia Woolf and the Bloomsbury set, right down to the TV executives, educationalists, civil servants, churchman and commentators of our own day, a thing tends to be preferred by virtue of it not being too overtly British. And of course, patriotism is simply beyond the pale, especially when it's expressed en masse. Cosmopolitan London, with its new status as a 'post-nation city', might be tolerable to this crowd. But the rest of the country is certainly not included in their view of what is desirable and to be celebrated.

These are the people who shape our culture, and with it much of the tone of public life. As a group they're given vague labels: they are variously the liberal elites, or the metropolitan elites, or – imaginatively – the liberal metropolitan elites. It might seem a crude way of classifying such apparently disparate groups; they do not carry membership cards, or all belong to some club. But we tend to know what we mean when we talk about them. Like the line about the sausage, it's hard quite to define it, but you know it when you see it.

A new establishment

It was on this already fertile ground that a new establishment rose up. This establishment was quite unlike the old one
which had been mocked to death by the end of the 1960s,
the decade of satire and *That Was the Week That Was*. Much
of it had its worldview formed in that same decade, the one
characterised by the French student protests of May 1968 and
the rise of the New Left. And it was an outlook which was
predominantly countercultural, which is to say, not one in
which pride in a nation or its history figured, other than as
punch lines to bad jokes.

The sons and daughters of the 1960s and the grim decade
which followed went on, in many respects, to run the show.
That is not to say that the new establishment is still full of
ex-student revolutionaries all champing at the bit to get to
the barricades. Far from it – many of those who now stalk the
corridors of power are perfectly happy with what capitalism
has to offer. As Peter Mandelson said about New Labour,
they can be 'intensely relaxed about people getting filthy rich'.
Few of the people who came to maturity during the 1960s
and who might retain a nostalgia for the upheavals of that
decade would now actively advocate a socialistic economic
system. That particular god failed, spectacularly and indeed
murderously. And neither do they necessarily want to break
up all of Britain's traditional institutions or ways of doing
things – not all of them anyway.

Rather, it is something more nuanced than that: the
economic backbone of their beliefs might have been broken,
but it left them with a set of views, attitudes and ways of

looking at things which were not shaken off when they should've been. They have continued to inform the priorities of many of those who inhabit the various peaks in our society and what they seek to do, and have in turn shaped Britain.

Chief amongst these was a belief and adherence to cultural relativism. Whenever we bemoan the apparent inability of our society to assert the difference between right and wrong, or stand firmly behind one way of doing things rather than another, it can be traced back to the influence of cultural relativism. At its centre was a belief that there was no such thing as absolute truth, that all cultures were of equal worth, and that right and wrong existed only within the boundaries of any one specific society and should in no way be judged.

This was to have a profound effect on Britain when it had become multicultural in a way which simply couldn't have been imagined forty years ago. But also, by its very nature it tended to inhibit the holding of a belief which saw Britain as having great and distinctive features – or for that matter, being responsible for achievements which could be appreciated as beneficial to the entire world.

Them

The views and values of the elites are more often than not hugely at variance with the vast bulk of the population.

Take the monarchy, while we're being topical. Opinion polls taken over a period of forty years have shown that the percentage of people in favour of the institution, and wishing it to continue, has stayed remarkably static, at around 70 to 75 per cent. Similarly the percentage supporting an end to the

Crown and its replacement by a presidential system rarely goes above 20 per cent. During the difficult years of the 1990s, and especially during the extraordinary period after the death of Diana, the anti-monarchist percentage rose to about a third of those asked, but this dropped back to the usual level remarkably quickly after the Queen made her broadcast to the nation and started to bring the volatile situation around.

As was pointed out by Roger Mortimore, MORI's director of political analysis, support for the monarchy was probably the most stable trend his polling company had ever measured. It could therefore be classified as a 'value' – slow to change, and powerful – rather than a more moveable opinion or attitude.

But didn't you think that the monarchy was finished? Of course you did, because isn't that what everyone's sort of saying? Well, certainly in large sections of the media they were saying it relentlessly at one point. The fact is that republican sentiment is disproportionately higher in the print and broadcast media, as it is within much of the new establishment in general. Certainly the movers and shakers of north London find it impossible to take seriously.

They are entitled to their views of course, it's a free country etc., etc. But the crucial point is that these people have a far greater access to influence and opinion-forming than the country at large. Sure enough, it was they who declared (with some gleeful wishful thinking no doubt) that the Golden Jubilee in 2002 would be a huge flop, that nobody cared about the death of the Queen Mother, and that William and Kate's wedding would be a shadow of that of his parents. Each time they said the same thing, and each time they got it badly wrong. They were genuinely baffled at the sight of hundreds of thousands pouring into London to cheer or pay their respects. Gazing at the world from the windows of metropolitan media clubs might give one a distorted view. Who *were* all these people?

Us

The monarchy is just one example. As we've already seen, the liberal elites were always far more supportive of the European Union, in some cases slavishly so. This was often just as much based on their general dismissal of much of British culture and disproportionate enthusiasm for the European variety as it was on any passionately held belief in a single currency. But it does not stop there: on a whole spread of issues, from discipline in schools through to immigration, there is a major, yawning chasm between what used to be called the silent majority and those who set the boundaries of debate.

Some topics can actually be made into non-issues. Capital punishment is an instance of this. For what it's worth I am not in favour of it. But you can disagree with what is apparently still the majority view (pro) and yet feel disquiet at the way in which it has become off-limits as a subject for public discussion. As with other issues, it has been simply 'disappeared'.

Views and topics can be driven to the periphery by making supporters feel not just that they are wrong, but actually bad people. It means that you do not have to answer their points; you can simply dismiss them *ad hominem* and retain a nice, warm sense of your own moral superiority. As we shall see later, the same applies to multiculturalism. This was such a binding article of faith that anybody who thought that we might be stacking up problems for the future, or simply disagreed with the whole premise, could be branded if not evil then certainly outside the boundaries of reasonable society. As such, they shouldn't be listened to.

There was the most perfect example of this during the 2010 general election. While on the campaign trail the then Prime Minister, Gordon Brown, found himself having a for-once-unscripted and unexpected exchange with an ordinary voter, Gillian Duffy, who was concerned about the high levels of immigration in her area. She asked the PM, in moderate, concerned and friendly terms (she was a Labour supporter) what he was going to do about it. Brown mumbled something placatory, and, obviously embarrassed, couldn't get away quick enough. Having rather stupidly left his microphone on, he complained to an aide about the incident as he was driven away, before dismissing Mrs Duffy as just 'a bigot'. This got the PM into seriously hot water later on, when his comment was played back to him on a radio show.

It was a very revealing moment, in that it showed his contempt for the voter and the concerns she voiced. But the truth is, Brown's attitude, and his private response, was not particular to him. It was in fact the authentic voice of the political class, the liberal establishment, that we heard that day. Mrs Duffy's questions were not worthy of a response; she could be dismissed on the grounds of her assumed character. The attitude he expressed towards her was one commonly found within the world in which he moved. In being caught out, Brown just happened to be the unlucky one.

What, though, has this got to do with British identity, or national pride? The truth is, it has everything to do with it. There is the basic point of principle that in a country such as Britain, which has always treasured freedom of speech as one of its defining values, people should be able to feel that they can express their views without their characters being called into question or possibly, as in the case of Mrs Duffy, even slandered. This principle is being undermined on an almost daily basis now. Alongside it comes a withering of the idea that Britain has something unique in its traditions – freedom of speech – which singles it out from many nations.

But there is a wider issue here. Just as they have unquestioningly supported multiculturalism, the political class and the liberal elites also feel queasy when it comes to expressions of national pride, or anything they sense is too nation-centric.

There can, for example, be no other explanation for the criticism of the popular Prom concerts, by the then culture minister Margaret Hodge, as not promoting the 'right kind' of Britishness. This inhibition was also behind the gargantuan levels of hype behind Britain's winning bid for the Olympics in 2012: in the initial stages at least, the political class felt much easier about supporting this piece of expensive international pageantry than they did the Diamond Jubilee, which might have struck them as too home-grown, too organically British, and therefore slightly embarrassing.

The basic position is to find patriotism either silly and, if you're a certain type of Tory, a bit downmarket, or suspect and, if you're a certain type of left-winger, dangerous.

So it isn't a Left/Right thing?

The two World Wars certainly left European countries with a fear of anything that could be described as nationalism. Patriotism can be held distinct from nationalism because traditionally the latter was aggressive, possibly bellicose and certainly exclusive. It was seen as basically a destructive force, which worked against any efforts towards increased international understanding. Patriotism on the other hand, being defined as a love for one's country, its history and institutions, did not by necessity involve hatred towards others, nor did it thrive on exclusivity.

So, theoretically, you can, for example, be a Conservative and be very wary of nationalism, or a Labour supporter with a very strong sense of national pride. But I use the term Labour supporter advisedly here. For there is no question that in the period since the Second World War, the broader political Left – not necessarily to be found in the Labour party – has mounted a sustained assault on Britain and Britishness.

As we saw earlier, in the modern era this war had its origins in the upheavals of the 1960s, the emergence of the hard-line New Left and a counterculture which, eventually, was to become the mainstream. All traditions and established ways had to be not just questioned but up-ended or abolished, simply on the basis that they had been existing for years. There was no thought as to their efficiency or effectiveness – the destruction was meted out simply on the principle that old must in some way be bad, corrupt or hypocritical.

Our institutions – church, police, Parliament – had to be shown to be oppressors, the pedlars of outdated morality, innately reactionary, and certainly not on our side. Our history had to be shown as a series of unrelentingly dark, disgusting deeds of which we should be ashamed. As a past imperial power, the world's problems could be put firmly at our door. Britain's very sense of identity had to be deconstructed. And in ushering in multiculturalism and its implicit attack on the 'dominant culture', the Left scored its biggest success.

What is remarkable is that there was virtually no real opposition to these developments. Most Conservatives – or the parliamentary variety at least – ceded all the ground to their opponents, inch by inch, and essentially acquiesced to the new terms of debate. This was true even during the Thatcher era: the Prime Minister was, as it were, away fighting the crusades in the economic war of that decade, leaving the cultural one unfought by colleagues who, believing they didn't have right on their side, did not have the stomach for the battle. Thus today, on so many cultural and social issues, there is virtually nothing of real difference between Labour and Tory.

The science bit

Rudi Dutschke, one of the leaders of the Leftist student movement in Germany in the late 1960s, coined a phrase, 'The Long March through the Institutions'. Like his comrades-in-arms in France and Britain, he was heavily influenced by the writing of Antonio Gramsci, an early twentieth-century Italian Marxist who, put very simply, believed that for a revolution to succeed, the culture of a country had to be infiltrated and captured – a view which was based on the belief that the proletariat could not be sufficiently relied upon to rise up on its own in the way originally prescribed by Marx.

This long march would then create another type of 'consciousness' – not the supposedly 'false' one under which workers had hitherto laboured – which would in turn facilitate the ultimate, revolutionary change in society which they craved and which they believed in with all the fervour of religious fundamentalists patiently awaiting Armageddon. In effect, it would bring about the revolution from within.

Did the Left of the 1960s take Gramsci at his word? Was there 'a long march'? We are not talking here of some kind of grand, organised conspiracy, some sort of deliberate, systematically carried out plan of action. Developments in history always tend to be much more shambolic than that. But what cannot be doubted is that the Left of the 1960s – the people who in France are known as the 'Sixty-Eighters' – left a profound mark on most of the countries in which they were active. The academic, educational, and cultural fields became dominated by a set of left-of-centre beliefs which have influenced the way we've run things ever since.

At a day-to-day level, this has made itself felt in the shifting leftwards of what became known as the 'centre ground' in politics, and, in a wider context, in what was henceforth considered reasonable, moderate opinion. Socialism was, naturally, the future, so anybody who opposed this obvious societal progression, however moderately, was automatically a dyed-in-the-wool reactionary and not to be taken seriously (even the Tory party seemed to accept this analysis for much of the post-war period). Just to take one example, the desirability of universal welfare systems was accepted as a given, with those who might have considered it harmful or damaging regarded as off-the-radar right wing (an attitude which has only very recently showed serious signs of changing).

But it went further than this. Cultural attitudes, even personal attributes, were increasingly characterised along political lines ('the personal is political' was one of the more hackneyed mantras of the 1960s and 1970s). A belief in personal resourcefulness, for example, became evidence of a 'right-wing' mentality. Similarly, supporting discipline in schools (or even in the home) was recategorised as a 'conservative' position. The truth of course is that there is nothing inherently right or left wing in either resourcefulness or discipline (socialist activists had once traditionally been characterised by both), but in the post-countercultural world, everything was fair game for politicisation. And without question, patriotism, or a strong identification with one's country, were – when viewed from this 'moderate' civilised centre-ground – roundly labelled right-wing attributes.

Guilty! Guilty! Guilty?

Perhaps one of the greatest triumphs of the post-war left was instilling an overpowering sense of national guilt into their respective societies: guilt for past sins, whether real or imagined, guilt for simply being British, or French, or Dutch. We still live with this today.

When he was elected President of France, Nicolas Sarkozy declared his intention to rid the country of its habit of repenting for its 'sins'. 'This repentance,' he said, 'is a form of self-hatred.' For him, the near-revolutionary upheavals of 1968 represented moral relativism and social anarchy, and the destruction of social and patriotic values. This spirit lived on, he said, in the leftist heirs to that era, but its overwhelmingly harmful effect on society 'must be liquidated once and for all'.

Whatever else we might think of Mr Sarkozy, about this he was absolutely right. French politicians are quite happy to talk about such issues, and their choice of words is often refreshingly blunt. It is a pity that it has been so, so rare to hear anything remotely similar from any of our own leaders.

In his 2006 book *La Tyrannie de la Pénitence* (The Tyranny of Guilt), the prominent French philosopher Pascal Bruckner argued that this guilt had become pathological in the West, and was actually now an obstacle to constructive action in situations where it was needed. All modern thought, he wrote, 'can be reduced to a mechanical denunciation of the West, emphasising the latter's hypocrisy, violence, and abomination'. He went on:

In this enterprise the best minds have lost much of their substance. Few of them have avoided succumbing to this spiritual routine: one applauds a religious revolution, another goes into ecstasies over the beauty of terrorist acts or supports a guerrilla movement because it challenges our imperialist project. Indulgence towards foreign dictatorships, intransigence towards our democracies ... the duty to repent forbids the Western bloc, which is eternally guilty, to judge or combat other systems, other states, other religions. Our past crimes command us to keep our mouths closed. Our only right is to remain silent.

French politicians and philosophers, we can see, regard this as an issue which can and should be openly discussed. Yet here in Britain, which arguably has one of the worse self-induced cases of guilt and self-loathing in the Western world, barely a word is mentioned. Instead it is allowed to run unchecked like poison through our system; it's there, in the air we breathe every day, yet remains virtually unopposed.

In his excellent essay 'Table Manners', Tony Wells describes an all too typical scenario – a middle-class dinner party of academics, publishers and the like, at which he made the cardinal error of referring to Britain and the West as advanced societies. He was immediately upbraided for his use of the word 'advanced' by a guest who took offence on behalf of those not even at the table:

> The suspicion has to be, of course, that my dinner companions are frightened by the consequences of accepting that we are an advanced society; frightened by the responsibility it brings. For if we embrace our liberties, and the institutions that guarantee them, as advanced, and take pride in them, we must by implication believe that other nations and peoples would benefit from copying them... If I think the freedom of speech, conscience and expression enjoyed by the British and others is a good thing, I must consider them a good thing for everyone, and not just for the British.

As we shall see further on, all of this has had enormous consequences not just for the way in which our history is taught (or not), but it also accounts for the pervasive air of apology that clings to even a simple admission of one's nationality. It ignores completely, indeed will not even acknowledge, any of Britain's (or the West's) remarkable achievements. It is rather like summing up an individual's character and life with reference only to his faults. So, it has become much easier instead to overcompensate by either adopting an uncritical, almost sycophantic approach to any culture other than one's own or, as Bruckner pointed out, by keeping your mouth shut.

We are all victims now

Another, not unrelated political dogma which emerged from that wonderful decade known as the 1960s was to have huge consequences, not just for the way in which we see ourselves, but for the very notion of society as something which was collectively experienced.

So-called identity politics, by which individuals were encouraged to see themselves first and foremost as a woman, or a gay man, or a person from an ethnic minority, ran completely counter to the traditional way of identifying oneself as belonging to a much wider grouping of people, with habits, history and location in common – a nation, for example. The effect of identity politics was to slice through society, creating horizontal and vertical lines which separated people out on the basis of one particular aspect of their being – whether it be their sexuality, say, or race. This was then held up as the defining quality of that individual, from which everything else flowed.

Needless to say, a sense of national identity was way, way down the list according to this set of priorities. If you doubt this, then just try to imagine a member of the public being interviewed on the television news and starting, 'Well, as a British man, I feel that...' We would find it slightly corny, slightly embarrassing now (old newsreels reveal that it was not always so). Identity politics went so far into the mainstream that now, we longer even really notice it.

Of course, it also created lots of little prisons for the unwitting who took this approach to heart, gloried in it, and then found that they couldn't really move without their actions being explained (and more often, excused) on the basis of one of their characteristics. For there was one important aspect to this new way of identifying ourselves that was finally to have a hugely deleterious effect on morale, whether personal or national: it was based on a notion that these groups were victims.

Richard Bernstein, the *New York Times*' culture correspondent and author of *Dictatorship of Virtue*, explained this victimhood culture succinctly in an important 1990 article:

> Central to pc-ness, which has its roots in 1960s radicalism, is the view that Western society has for centuries been dominated by what is often called 'the white male power structure' or 'Patriarchal hegemony'. A related belief is that everybody but white heterosexual males has suffered some form of repression and been denied a cultural voice.

It didn't really matter that some of the grievances on which this sense of victimhood was encouraged might have been real and valid at some point. What mattered more was that it had to be kept alive, regardless of any progress that might have been made in rectifying wrongs past or present. Kept alive and – if possible – expanded exponentially (one recent survey came up with the finding that over 70 per cent of British people could in one way or another classify themselves legitimately as victims).

The result has been that we live in a Britain which seems to be in a permanent state of anguish, in which problems are never solved, claims are never met, wrongs are never righted, and in which there is endless, endless, endless complaining.

You can't say that!

If, however, you want to answer these complaints, you better use the right language. By which I mean, of course, with the acceptable forms of communication which have been laid down by a code which now defines how we interact: political correctness.

PC, as it is known, is an odd phenomenon in that while it is the butt of jokes and almost universally reviled – you will rarely come up against somebody who is willing to defend it – it is also now universally adhered to. How this translates in everyday life is that people are aware enough of its strictures to begin a conversation with the caveat 'I know this might not be very politically correct, but…' usually followed by a perfectly reasonable point which is characterised simply by the fact of it being a personally stated opinion. They start this way, however, because they are aware that they might be told that something is now deemed unsayable, and are wary of the responses of strangers. 'You can't say that!' has, appallingly, become one of the most familiar twenty-first-century phrases.

As with many theories which become horribly distorted in practice, PC had some honourable intentions, perhaps, in the beginning – the lessening of intolerance and discrimination. Some treated it as a sort of modern day version of Victorian euphemism, born of a desire to be polite and considerate. But as PC became more entrenched it became clear that its other purpose – to change circumstances by simply altering the way they could be described and discussed – was having an increasingly pernicious effect. Now, with PC dominant in all parts of our society, from television and films through to the civil service and, especially, the academic world, many people are genuinely unclear about what they can and cannot say.

But they instinctively know that encouraging traditional patriotism, or being too aware of one's national identity (at least when it comes to Britishness), is most definitely not part of PC's mission. The case mentioned earlier, of Margaret Hodge's intervention over the Proms, is a good example of how it works. Hodge complained about the lack of 'inclusiveness' which she discerned at this world-famous series of summer concerts. There are over fifty of these, but one couldn't help but assume that what bugged her most was the flag-waving ritual of the Last Night, and its customary patriotic songs, such as 'Land of Hope and Glory' and 'Jerusalem'. This was not, in her view, the kind of Britishness we should be promoting. It was possibly alienating, possibly actually offensive, to other groups.

On the face of it, Hodge's reasoning seemed well-intentioned: what could be bad about wanting to include more people? Wasn't this an example of a PC approach aiming for a positive effect? The reality, however, would mean the loss, or watering down, of a much-loved tradition enjoyed by millions of people every year, simply because of the perceived offence it might cause some. It didn't happen, as we know, but the minor storm created by her comments left a legacy, albeit unconsciously felt: her position was the PC one, the morally righteous one, so those who disagreed and were dismayed at her words must automatically be non-PC, and therefore one step away from being imperialist reactionary scumbags, if not already there.

As Anthony Browne pointed out in his sobering pamphlet for the Civitas think tank, 'The Retreat of Reason', there are countless other instances of PC in action which are more serious than the above example, in that it can get in the way of dealing with material life-and-death situations. So for example, the politically correct view of why Africa is getting poorer is that the West does not give enough economic aid, whereas the reality is that bad, corrupt governance throughout that continent is to blame. Similarly, the sudden and steep rise in HIV infection in heterosexuals in the UK is, according to the PC explanation, due to younger people having unsafe sex, whereas the fact is it has been largely fuelled by immigration from Africa.

The offence defence

In both these examples, we see guilt taking a hand – guilt in mentioning inconvenient truths. Much of the foreign aid industry relies on an underlying sense that in some way, we are to blame for the plight of the starving in Africa. Many of those working in this now heavily politicised field really do believe this (and believed it *before* they worked in it, not because of their subsequent experience), and while the majority of people are not convinced – a *Sunday Times* poll at the time of the much-hyped Live8 concert found that most people did indeed see bad governance as the main reason for African poverty – there is enough of a sense of guilt floating around for them not to challenge the PC-held truth.

PC is kept in place by its own system of checks and balances. It has a sort of penal code all of its own, which is based on the giving and taking of offence. There is, as yet, still no commandment which states that *'Thou Shalt Not Suffer Offence'*, but much of contemporary life now revolves around a fear of possibly upsetting some group or individual, a very hazardous situation considering that the numbers just waiting to take offence seem to be growing by the day.

Most of us are familiar with the stream of tabloid stories that describe instances of political correctness 'gone mad' – when, as the columnist Richard Littlejohn puts it, 'you couldn't make it up'. There's no doubt that many of these wackier stories about piggy banks being banned and blackboards giving offence are embellished and sensationalised, and that the truth, when one looks closer, is a little more nuanced. But it is nevertheless undeniable that a strong, overweening PC sensibility took root at the heart of public life, and now acts successfully to inhibit formal debate, quash informal everyday discussion and, if necessary, ostracise those it considers guilty.

The main point is that the giving of offence appears to be a one-way street. When it is said that offence might be given to an array of ethnic groups by the putting up of a Union flag, or the holding of a Christmas fair might alienate Muslims, it is hardly surprising that most people register such expressions of 'sensitivity' as an attack on their own traditions and culture. And they are, for the most part, right, for the thinking of those who pride themselves on such sensitivity is more often than not grounded in distaste for those traditions and that culture. Confirmation of this is to be found in the fact that the very groups they presume to be protecting are often not remotely offended, and are bemused at what is being done supposedly for their benefit.

The voice of Britain?

Political correctness continues to provide a fund of sometimes amusing but mostly exasperating stories for parts of the British media. Not, however, for our national broadcaster, for it is at the BBC that the preoccupations and priorities of the elites can be found in all their glory.

The issue of the BBC worldview, and the influence it has on our culture, has become much more widely discussed in recent years. Certainly when it comes to news coverage, both Tory and Labour politicians criticise the corporation over the way they are respectively reported, which its supporters suggest tends to show that it must be getting something right, and that it is not, as is often claimed, inherently anti-Conservative in its outlook. But this is to look at it rather narrowly. When Labour is criticised on the BBC, it tends to be from a left-wing position.

More fundamentally, the people who are drawn to work there are hugely more likely to be of a metropolitan left/liberal persuasion. Not for nothing has the BBC been called *The Guardian* of the Airwaves. Sir Anthony Jay, the creator of the classic comedy series *Yes Minister*, once described the attitudes of those he worked with when he first joined the corporation in the Macmillan era:

> We were not just anti-Macmillan; we were anti-industry, anti-capitalism, anti-advertising, anti-selling, anti-profit, anti-patriotism, anti-monarchy, anti-Empire, anti-police, anti-armed forces, anti-bomb, anti-authority. Almost anything that made the world a freer, safer and more prosperous place, you name it, we were anti it.

Time might have moved on, and the BBC – still seen to an extent by the rest of the world as the country's voice – has been forced to admit that on certain issues, such as the European Union, where in its reporting the corporation's Europhilia was virtually undisguised, there might have been a problem. Mark Thompson, the out-going director-general, has also accepted the existence of an anti-Thatcher bias in the 1980s. But the recent memoirs of the former BBC newsreader Peter

Sissons confirmed that, in all its essentials, the basic mindset outlined by Jay, remains very much in place.

'What the BBC regards as normal and abnormal, what is moderate or extreme, where the centre of gravity of an issue lies,' wrote the veteran BBC man Michael Buerk recently, 'are conditioned by the common set of assumptions held by the people who work for it… *The Guardian* is their bible and political correctness their creed.'

How much damage has this done to British culture? It is near impossible to measure in any scientific way. But unquestionably, the effect of years of chipping away at our view of ourselves, of sowing doubt about our actions and our institutions, must surely have had an enormous effect on national morale.

But wot about *The Sun*?

Those who disagree that our culture is dominated by a liberal-left sensibility usually point to large circulation newspapers like the *Daily Mail* and *The Sun* as being staunch, tub-thumping defenders of all things British, who can be relied upon jingoistically to run up the flag on the flimsiest of excuses. These chauvinistic rags are the most read papers in Britain, they cry.

It is undeniable that these titles loom large and carry with them a fair amount of political influence, although this always tends to be overstated, not least by politicians themselves, and is in any case in decline as readership of papers in general gives way to the fragmented internet. But they are taken seriously as a reflection of the views of their readers, and as such, are certainly important features on the cultural landscape.

But the fact remains that, compared to the small but highly influential readership of *The Guardian*, readers of *The Sun* and *Mail* possess very little access to power, and can bring little to bear on the general direction of our culture. Their readers are not, broadly speaking, in a position to formulate an educational policy, or stop the growth of European federalism, or challenge institutionalised multiculturalism. The papers themselves react to this, which might account for the level of frustration and anxiety that permeate their editorials.

The world represented by the *Mail* and *The Sun*, and the presumed views and instincts of their readers, are not sanctioned as part of our culture by our elites. Far from it. They are there to be mocked, to be used as a shorthand for all sorts of undesirable and unwholesome opinions, and their readers caricatured and ridiculed. The quickest way for a left-wing comedian on a BBC panel show to get a derisive laugh is to smirk at the '*Daily Mail* reader', or the even more condescending 'white van man'. The concerns felt by these groups – that Britain is going to hell and they are powerless to do anything about it – is treated equally scornfully.

David Cameron's pronouncement, after becoming Tory leader, that he liked Britain the way it is now might have had much to do with repositioning the supposedly polluted Conservative 'brand', but it could equally have been a sincerely held belief. If the latter, then he would simply have been giving voice to the authentic viewpoint of much of the new establishment (and as such, might have permanently alienated many voters who would've been wondering what planet he was living on). There is a cultural consensus now, every bit as strong as the economic one used to be in the years before Thatcher, and the political class whether Left, Right or indifferent have signed up to it. But the truth is, the rarefied atmosphere in which the establishment operates exists a thousand miles away from the everyday experiences of millions of people, whose fears and concerns about the state and fate of the country exist largely theoretically, out there, beyond the metropolitan bubble.

CHAPTER THREE

FORGETTING OURSELVES

A few years ago, George Courtauld, a City headhunter, was travelling home on the train through the Essex countryside. He witnessed something which was eventually to inspire a minor publishing sensation.

'There was a little boy with his arm in a sling looking for a seat next to his friends,' he explained in a later interview with the *Daily Telegraph*. 'A kindly older woman offered him hers, suggesting that "little Lord Nelson" might like to sit.

'But the boy did not know whom the woman was talking about. She said: "You know, England expects! Admiral Nelson."

'And the boy replied: "Of course, the man in *Star Trek*!"'

Struck by the boy's ignorance of one of Britain's great heroes, Courtauld wrote out a list of important events in history which he thought his own children should know about, and pinned it to the loo door. The enthusiasm for the list shown by friends and relations led him to expand the idea; he spent six months researching what was to become known as *The Pocket Book of Patriotism*, a slim volume which he later described as 'a very simple history book. No judgement, no padding – just the bare bones of our magnificent history.'

Courtauld was definitely onto something, but the distinct lack of interest from the publishers he approached meant that, with some backing from friends, he ended up publishing 10,000 copies himself. Some of the publishers had even suggested he take out certain elements in the book, such as the flags, and the Churchill speeches, and change the title. 'Everyone seemed concerned about the Britishness of it all,' he said. 'Patriotism nowadays seems to be linked with terrible movements like the BNP.'

It is, unfortunately, hardly surprising that publishers didn't want it; along with so many in what are known as the creative industries, they tend to be of a distinctly *Guardian*-esque hue. But despite this early lack of help, the book simply took off. Within the first week he had taken 26,000 orders for it. Eventually, the big bookselling chains began to stock it.

'I really thought I'd sell 200 copies and that would be it,' he said. 'When I sold 1,000 books at the launch party, I was surprised. I didn't for one minute think I would shift the 10,000 copies I originally printed, let alone in four days.'

At just sixty-four pages, *The Pocket Book of Patriotism* went on to become a runaway bestseller, and eventually a beautifully illustrated edition was published. But in essence it is exactly as Courtauld described it – little more than a clear, concise timeline of British history, from Stonehenge down to the beginning of the second millennium, with no exposition or commentary. Along with segments of famous speeches and pictures of the flags of the UK, there are the words to national songs such as 'Jerusalem', and – in a move which probably irritated those publishers – he also included lists of imperial weights and measures, and all the territories of the British Empire as it stood in 1920. But in some ways, the title was a misnomer, for the book didn't set out to list all Britain's great achievements. It wasn't so much a book of patriotism as a reference book of facts about Britain's past.

Desperately seeking dates...

The success of Courtauld's book showed the extent of public demand for the simplest of information about our national story, ones that could be handed down to a younger generation. This should not come as a surprise to anyone, when one looks at the level of ignorance about important people and events in British history. A number of surveys carried out in recent years have produced sobering results, amongst which are the following:

- A fifth of British teenagers thought that Winston Churchill was a fictional character.
- 47 per cent of the same sample (of 3,000) thought that Richard the Lionheart was similarly made up.
- 27 per cent thought that Florence Nightingale was, likewise, a mythical character.
- One in ten adults thought Hitler didn't really exist.
- One in five thought that Harold Wilson was Prime Minister during the Second World War.
- One in seven did not know that the Battle of Hastings was real, more than half thought that Nelson was in charge at

Waterloo, and around a quarter didn't know than Trafalgar was a real battle. Three-quarters did not know that the Battle of Blenheim took place 300 years ago.

- 30 per cent of 11- to 18-year-olds thought that Oliver Cromwell fought at the Battle of Hastings.
- A similar figure did not know in which century the First World War took place.
- Almost half of adults thought William Wallace was fictional.

These are truly depressing findings. However, a strong element of surreal humour creeps in when we see that the same surveys found an often widespread belief that certain famous mythical, literary and pop culture fictional figures actually existed. Fifty-eight per cent of teens thought that Sherlock Holmes was a real person, as did a full 65 per cent for King Arthur. It starts to get really tragic, however, when we find that 1 in 20 adults thought that the Arnold Schwarzenegger movie hero Conan the Barbarian was real; some thought the same of Xena: Warrior Princess and even Lord Blackadder.

Confusion reigns

Certainly, people have never been so soaked in a constant stream of seven-days-a-week, round-the-clock entertainment as they are now, so to take the charitable view, it's never been *so* possible to become, well, a bit confused about what's real and what isn't. There are still the misguided souls here and there who think soap characters are real, so the same must happen with history. But this doesn't go very far in explaining the serious gaps in very basic knowledge amongst large sections of the population which these surveys show, or for that matter, the complete lack of any sense of the chronology of our national story. The past is regarded almost as a junkyard of different unrelated styles, objects and people.

My own experience bears this out. A twenty-year-old friend of my young niece, quite a bright guy, was nevertheless under the impression, it became clear during a conversation, that Henry VIII was succeeded on the throne by Queen Victoria. It's hard to know where to start here but surely, at the most superficial level, dress style alone would tell you that these two people must be centuries apart. And even when there is at least a rudimentary historical awareness, the conclusions drawn can still be alarmingly distorted. None of this is their fault of course; it is the way they have been taught, or not taught.

That same niece, as an early teen, was once looking through my mother's photo albums. She came across a group school picture from the 1940s. 'But where are all the black people?' she enquired earnestly. Before we could tell her about the *Windrush*, and that immigration on a large scale happened a little later on, she answered her own question: 'Oh yes, that's right, there was segregation wasn't there?' This was quite chilling, that she could run away with such an idea. But the fact that she had put two and two together and made five derived solely from the way she had been taught history: as a series of single projects, just topics without any chronology – the Nazis, the US Civil Rights movement, the Pyramids.

Quite recently I found myself arguing with a young twenty-something who was convinced that in reality Germany had won the Second World War, because they were now the most prosperous country in Europe and we were, as he put it, a basket case. The last part of that statement is indeed an arguable one; but he'd arrived at it by seeing the war in solely economic terms. 'But the point of the war was to stop Hitler, and for that matter, Hitler invading us!' I said, trying to hide my exasperation and at the same time not look like Captain Mainwaring. 'Oh yeah, well, if you put it like that, then yeah, I see what you mean,' came the reply.

Losing our memory

Of course Courtauld's book was not the first one to major on famous dates. The humorous classic from 1930 by Sellar and Yeatman, *1066 and All That*, which also concerned itself with the most important points in our history, gratuitously jumbled up important facts and famous names to great comic effect. But the humour derived from the assumption that the readers knew the basic facts. It's probable now that *1066 and All That* would be taken at face value by many people.

Not knowing about our past makes us unknowable to ourselves. As the historian Simon Schama once said

Who is it that needs history the most? Our children, of course: the generations who will either pass on the memory of our disputatious liberty or be not much bovvered about the doings of obscure ancestors, and go back to Facebook for an hour or four. Unless they can be won to history, their imagination will be held hostage in the cage of eternal Now: the flickering instant that's gone as soon as it has arrived. They will thus remain, as Cicero warned, permanent children, for ever innocent of whence they have come and correspondingly unconcerned or, worse, fatalistic about where they might end up... The seeding of amnesia is the undoing of citizenship.

Schama – who could hardly be classified as a reactionary historian of the Sir Bufton Tufton school – was absolutely right. Much of our culture now is indeed held in 'the cage of eternal Now', as we shall explore later on. Are we in danger of completely losing our national memory?

Certainly what we are faced with now is a situation where within many parts of the state educational system, history has been allowed to wither away. An all-party parliamentary report found last year that History was increasingly concentrated in private and grammar schools. In 2010, fewer than one in three 16-year-olds in the comprehensive state system were entered for History GCSE, compared to the 55 per cent entered in grammar schools. In 2011, no pupils at all were entered for GCSE History in 159 schools. In Knowsley on Merseyside, eleven out of a possible 2,000 pupils took A level history (and only four of these passed).

History has been discouraged, along with other serious subjects, in favour of the lightweight, which in turn has helped keep the results up when it comes to the all-important league tables. Many have put the blame at the door of the National Curriculum. 'The syllabus has been a shambles for years,' the historian Dominic Sandbrook has said. 'Fragmented and fractured, obsessed with the Nazis and apparently indifferent to the pleasures of narrative, it leaves students struggling for a sense of the contours of our national story.'

The current Education Secretary, Michael Gove, who seems to be alone in the current government in understanding that these are the sort of vitally important cultural battles that need to be won, has likewise condemned the way history has been taught. 'Most parents would rather their children had a traditional education, with children sitting in rows, learning the kings and queens of England,' he said in 2012. Most parents probably did indeed breathe a sigh of relief at hearing that. But the task faced by Gove or for that matter anyone wanting to take on the notoriously left-wing educational establishment is fearsome; it would essentially be the cultural version of Thatcher's battle with the miners.

... or having it rubbed out?

In the post-war decades the whole direction of education changed from one of the gaining of knowledge and literacy to a preoccupation with social engineering, and changing British society. Matters of class, gender and ethnicity took precedence and informed the way in which educationalists across the board saw themselves and their roles. Leading the onslaught was a political and intellectual class which was mired in self-loathing and shame, especially for Britain's imperial past.

As Melanie Phillips wrote in her brilliant dissection of Britain's derelict education system *All Must Have Prizes*:

Instead of transmitting the national culture, [education] was now to be used to correct people's prejudices. The system was therefore to be turned from the repository of disinterested knowledge to a vehicle for political and ideological propaganda. Instead of fostering the development of decent human beings by teaching them to think critically and independently on the basis of evidence laid out before them, it was now enjoined to produce or eliminate certain attitudes. Instead of teaching children how to think, it was to tell them what to think. To ensure that pupils emerged with the right attitudes, the cultural traditions had to be disavowed and supplanted by others.

The very nature of history meant it would be a particular target. British history could not be taught in a way which celebrated its past achievements. Indeed it could not be taught in a way which was not at the least even-handed about its good and bad points. For some time it was taught by the so-called Empathy method, which simply required pupils to put themselves in the position of, say, a worker during the industrial revolution or a medieval peasant. An interesting exercise for them no doubt, but such subjectivity is of little real ultimate value to them.

It's not surprising therefore that most young people, if indeed they have much of an idea about their country's history, have a vaguely negative feeling about what went on before they were born. They will have little or no notion of what the British Empire was, and how such a small, unpromising set of islands came to dominate a quarter of the world's surface and population, for good or ill. They will have no sense of the fact that Britain shaped the modern world.

Rather, they will – if they have any sense of their forebears at all – carry with them a sense that they have something to be ashamed about. 'The casual acceptance and systematic propagation of the claim that our own history and culture are somehow vicious and inferior at all times is bizarre,' wrote the bestselling historian Michael Burleigh.

> It is self-evident that the West generally, and Britain in particular, are responsible for many noble things and for much of what makes life in the modern world more agreeable than life in the thirteenth century. This does not mean, of course, that there is nothing to criticise; however, such criticism long ago lost all sense of proportion.

This negativity is reinforced long after the school bell has rung. A recent example was seen with the various celebrations held in 2007 to mark the 200th anniversary of the Act of Parliament which abolished slavery. The evils of slavery were described and rightly condemned; but little space was given to the campaign which led to its abolition, or indeed that it was a British parliament that passed the act. Even less attention was given to the fact that it was the British Navy who then policed the global seas to enforce the abolition. The emphasis was primarily on slavery as a terrible sin for which, by implication, we should all still be ashamed; the idea that we should take pride in having brought it to an end, as a result of enlightened thinking and the goodness and courage of figures such as William Wilberforce, was on the whole neglected.

In the introduction to his book *Empire: How Britain Made the Modern World*, the historian Niall Ferguson quotes from a BBC website which was aimed at school children. This was how it summed up Britain's imperial past:

> The Empire came to greatness by killing lots of people less sharply armed than themselves and stealing their countries, although their methods later changed: killing lots of people with machine guns came to prominence as the army's tactic of choice... [It] ... fell to pieces because of various people like Mahatma Ghandi, heroic revolutionary protester, sensitive to the needs of his people.

No room for doubt there then.

Pass it on, boys, pass it on

Alan Bennett's enormously popular play *The History Boys*, which had as its message the need to keep history and culture alive – a noble task – was seen by some commentators as a conservative play. The pupils were encouraged to resist the new-fangled ideas of a young teacher who taught controversy at all costs. This character was seen as an attack on some of the television historians then coming to prominence, and who in Bennett's eyes were destructive.

But the reality was, interestingly, the absolute reverse: the historians Bennett was taking a swipe at were for the most part those attempting to give some balance to the orthodox, negative mainstream history which, as we've seen, was being pumped through the education system. And they were also responding to a popular demand from the public.

And this is one of the chief reasons to be hopeful about the survival of our national memory. History might be badly taught in our schools, and as an academic discipline in our universities it might have become completely mired in left-wing dogma (and as a History undergraduate I can attest to this: sometimes I felt like I had been parachuted behind enemy lines) but thankfully, Britain has one of the most thriving markets in popular history, and the greatest public interest in the subject, of any country in the world.

Not knowing about history is one thing; not wanting to know about it is quite another, and all the signs are that despite it being endlessly revised, reviled and even junked by those institutions whose whole point is actually to 'pass it on', British history has an enormous appeal for many ordinary people who have a thirst for knowledge about our national story.

History is *so* last century

This interest displays itself in a number of ways. On television, which is where most people get their information, historians have become well-known faces if not completely household names. Niall Ferguson, with his thankfully even-handed series on the British Empire and America; Andrew Roberts and his particular take on Churchill and Hitler; and David Starkey's numerous walks through the Tudor and monarchical landscapes have all been accompanied by books which go on to be bestsellers in a way that dustier academics can only dream of. The tone of Simon Schama's *History of Britain*, made to usher in the new millennium, might have been more in the orthodox vein, but it ended on a moving note of muted patriotism.

Before these programmes made the airwaves, some TV commissioners had decided that history was boring and that nobody was interested – a far more patronising attitude than that of Lord Reith and the paternalism of his desire to inform, educate and entertain. This was, we should remember, during the 1990s, the heady days of Cool Britannia, and the 'rebranding' of the nation as a modern, young country. Television was part of the creative industries, which were happy to be promoted as being on the cutting edge, the true spirit, of contemporary Britain. The arbitrary and essentially philistine nature of this attempt at modernisation for the sake of it was symbolised best by the much-loathed and disastrous changing of British Airways' colours from red white and blue to a bizarre mishmash of ugly patterns and colours more typical of a banana republic.

For happening, dynamic people then, history meant the old, uncool Britannia. But the success of a few TV programmes which had managed to slip through the net meant that eventually the penny dropped: this stuff was popular. As if to compensate for recent neglect, the BBC came up with its *100 Greatest Britons* series in 2002, in which contemporary public figures had to plead the cases of their chosen historical figures before a public poll put them in order of distinction. It proved enormously popular, with 1.6 million votes cast. By some distance Churchill came out as top dog, followed by Brunel, and perhaps with a nod to recent memory, Diana, Princess of Wales came third (a result almost inconceivable if the poll were held now). The successful format was then adopted by other countries, including Germany (which understandably omitted Hitler from the list of candidates). Since then, history in one shape or form has rarely been off the TV screen, ranging from straight biography through to the popular 'lifestyle' treatments which aim to give people an idea of what life was like for ordinary people in centuries past.

The popularity of British history with the public is reflected in other ways, albeit sometimes obliquely. The National Trust now has a membership of nearly four million, a staggering number, making it the largest voluntary body in the world. Visiting castles, stately homes and their increasingly sophisticated associated attractions is very much part of British leisure time. Popular history magazines such as *History Today* are long-standing fixtures on the news-stands. Feature films based on British history are consistent crowd-pullers. Elizabeth I has been portrayed so many times now she has almost a sub-genre of her own, but she is closely followed by Henry VIII and Victoria. Even the twentieth century is good box office, as has most recently been illustrated by *The Queen* and *The King's Speech*.

Don't look back

Some commentators are very sniffy about all this. TV and film history is often very dodgy when it comes to the facts, they say, and anyway isn't it all much more to do with silly, useless nostalgia, something which is the bane of British culture?

Certainly films play around with chronology. But they can be hugely important if they successfully capture a certain spirit or an overriding central idea about a time or person. The 1998 film *Elizabeth*, starring Cate Blanchett, is a good example: the director Shekhar Kapur took all sorts of liberties with dates, played up the importance of some characters and changed the motives of others. But the film's depiction of the danger that surrounded the new young queen, and its portrayal of the way in which she later consolidated her power by reinventing herself as the Virgin Queen, were superb and historically valid. Such films spark further interest, and at a time when this is the last thing being done in schools, we should be almost grateful for them for keeping awareness alive.

The criticism that all this interest amounts to little more than a longing for the past amongst the British is one usually made by the same sort of people who had such trouble filling the Millennium Dome with things visitors would actually want to see. Certainly, European friends of mine have often been perplexed and amused by the number of programmes on British TV dedicated to all aspects of the Second World War, although one can understand the French and Germans for not sharing the obsession. Generally, however, there is little to suggest that the British are any more nostalgic, purely for the sake of it, than other nationalities (nostalgia should not be confused with that rather melancholic but altogether different sense of loss which can be found in certain aspects of specifically English music and literature).

No culture that was so intent on marooning itself in the past could produce, for example, Britain's world-class rock and pop (John Lennon, it should be noted, came seventh in the BBC poll of Great Britons). And as was illustrated by the Labour election landslide which unceremoniously dumped Churchill in 1945, Britain can be remarkably unsentimental when it comes to moving forward.

No, the charge of nostalgia is yet another example of Britain beating itself with its own stick. The same Britons who accuse their countrymen of wallowing in their past would, as we shall explore later, also be the first to celebrate and defend the right of any other culture to 'maintain their traditions', and sense of history.

The book of the film of the nation

In front of me now I have the *Sunday Times* list of bestselling books for 5 February 2012. Three of the top ten hardbacks are in different ways history-related: one on nineteenth-century railways, one on a First World War horse (no doubt due to the popularity of the film *Warhorse*) and the third an official companion to the TV series about Edwardian country house life, *Downton Abbey*. Of the ten bestselling paperbacks, four are similarly themed, again with TV playing a big part: the memoirs of a 1950s midwife, the story of the Second World War Bletchley Park codebreakers, an account of how a British soldier infiltrated Auschwitz, and a biography of Wallis Simpson.

Given the context of official neglect and discouragement in our educational system, such interest on the part of the buying public is heartening. And there are other examples: 2011 saw the publication of *Made in Britain*, a sumptuously illustrated, straightforward and detailed account of British history and the people who made it, by Adrian Sykes. It was well received, and managed to get a commendation from the Prime Minister David Cameron, who called it a 'very nice, rather old-fashioned book' that he was reading with his children.

Elsewhere, a group of self-styled citizen historians, led by Dr John Hart, came together to produce the 'National CV', a novel way of recounting British history in the form of a curriculum vitae. Like George Courtauld's *The Book of Patriotism*, this 25-page document was the result of dismay at the poor teaching of history in schools, and aimed to present all the important facts and dates, as well as achievements – including many that most young people would have no idea about – in a fresh and celebratory way. And up and down the country, there are those 'little platoons', associations of individuals who as a labour of love attempt to keep alive their particular pieces of local history.

There are many people then who wish to keep our national memory in good working order. It is all the more shocking therefore that its importance to the present and future health of the country should have been allowed to have been so compromised. There are signs that the extent of the damage is gradually being realised, and small attempts to undo it are being made.

But the deconstruction, the cult of shame and the negativity that has ruled over the past four decades have all gone

very deep. As we shall see next, this has had enormous consequences not just for our own fund of knowledge, but for the
very cohesiveness of our society.

CHAPTER FOUR

BEING VIBRANT

Just before Christmas 2011 a new, one-act opera opened at Covent Garden. Called *Yes*, it was the brainchild of the commentator and playwright Bonnie Greer – known mostly for her appearances on the BBC's *Newsnight Review* arts show – and was an account put to music of her experiences in the run-up to her participation as a panellist on the now-famous edition of *Question Time* which featured the leader of the BNP, Nick Griffin.

As it happens, the opera was lousy. But what was interesting was the way in which it reiterated and reconfirmed a view of the British which had been doing the politically correct rounds for some time, and which was fast on its way to becoming the unchallengeable mainstream orthodoxy. In essence, this was that there was no such thing as an indigenous Brit, that we were a mongrel nation, the product of waves and waves of immigrants over the centuries.

This was rammed home throughout the performance. We saw Ms Greer – who acted as a kind of narrator to the piece

– calling a friend at the British Museum who confirmed that yes, there wasn't a British person who couldn't trace their ancestry back to an immigrant or an invader. Every so often, a young Muslim woman jumped on stage to educate the audience about each of the various waves of immigration into Britain over the centuries. Just in case we hadn't got the point yet, a large screen above the stage gradually filled with the names of all the groups who'd come, shaped Britain, and presumably made it what it is today.

This was all received by an audience which, even if they had qualms, wouldn't have dreamt of airing them. Metropolitan and *bien pensant*, it's more than likely that they were largely on Ms Greer's side anyway. But to those who might not have been, what this message ultimately amounted to was that millions and millions of people had been deluding themselves. They were not what they thought they were.

The opera didn't actually feature the final, notorious *Question Time*. Then, it hadn't taken much for Griffin to reveal himself for the buffoon that he was, the head of a political party which in all its values could not be less truly British if it tried. The vast majority of people are not stupid, and neither, despite what sections of the liberal elite might think, are they racist; they know what the BNP are about, which is why that party has made such little real political headway. There are countless ways to counter and discredit the arguments of such extremist groups.

But claiming that the story of the people born in these islands amounts to little more than that of a demographic mishmash, a hodge-podge, barely existing as an entity at all really, is surely not the way to go about it. Not only is it plain wrong, but it is an argument which certainly wouldn't be tolerated when applied to virtually any other society or culture on earth – certainly not by the very same people who make it here.

But it also redraws the lines of debate in an alarming and completely distorted way. If the only answer to people like the BNP is to deconstruct British identity totally and claim it as a myth, then where does that leave those people – the majority of the public, in fact – who wouldn't dream of voting BNP but instinctively find such a politically motivated recasting of their history objectionable? Can they too be labelled racist now?

Let's have a heated debate

It is ridiculous and insulting, but unfortunately the answer to that last question is yes. Any method which closes down meaningful discussion on any aspect of immigration will be used – indeed, has been used – mercilessly. The very words 'a proper public debate is needed', when used by a politician or commentator can usually be taken as a signal that the subject is about to be packed away again. The definition of 'racist' has been expanded and expanded to include, either explicitly or by implication, anybody who in any way questions the orthodoxies which have been firmly in place for decades now, but which have been particularly enforced in the past fifteen years or so: that Britain has been immeasurably enriched by immigration, both socially and economically; that multicultural diversity is a huge strength which should be celebrated;

and more recently, that Britain is and only ever was the sum of its immigrants.

Let's stay with the world of the arts for a moment. Ms Greer's effort was the latest in what has become a tradition of cultural offerings in Britain which effectively provide the window-dressing for the political received wisdom of our age. The arts, TV and film have in this respect become the providers of visual aids to the various presentations of the liberal establishment. Far from being edgy, thought-provoking, iconoclastic or genuinely challenging – in other words all the things they usually claim to be – they relentlessly toe the party line on issues such as multiculturalism and British identity. Indeed, much of their public funding has been based on their ability effectively to put multiculturalism into practice.

So, a mile or so from where I am now writing, there is a new exhibition at Tate Britain called 'Migrations', which aims to 'reveal how British art has been fundamentally shaped by successive waves of immigration over 500 years'. Now, nobody would question the fact that Britain has been the home of choice to foreign artists who have made their name here over the centuries, from Hans Holbein onwards (and downwards). But the arrival of a steady, relatively tiny stream of artists over centuries, however 'fundamentally' influential they might have been, cannot by any stretch of the imagination by attributed as a by-product of 'successive waves of immigration'.

The trenchant but clichéd use of language gives the game away; there is a political point being made here, one happily regurgitated by art critics who wouldn't dream of demurring.

The study of outside influence on British art is a very worth-while one and about as old as the hills, as any art historian will tell you. But that is quite different to attempting to link it somehow with mass movements of people into Britain.

Try to put together a list of TV dramas, films, novels or plays which hold multiculturalism up as a destructive, segre-gating force, or which question the whole premise of mass immigration. You will not get very far. In fact most people will not be able to come up with a single title. Should it matter? Yes, because these things are important in that they create the atmosphere in which we live and shape our reac-tions to events and issues around us. One play, Richard Bean's *England People Very Nice*, which caused a stir of controversy when it was produced at London's National Theatre, certainly raised the issue, coming to the conclusion that successive waves of immigrants had generally assimilated well but that there might be problems with contemporary, radical Islam. For this Bean was barracked by some activists when taking part in a discussion on stage. But even he had used an area of East London as the setting for his drama, a place which, with its particular history, could not fairly be described as typical of the whole country's experience. The overriding feeling one was left with was still that 'twas ever thus. And on televi-sion, the BBC's ongoing soap opera about the contemporary life of *EastEnders*, is little more than a polite fiction, a wish-fulfilment fantasy; the last time that the picture it portrays could claim to have had any basis in reality was the early 1980s, at the very latest.

The new orthodoxy – that Britain is a nation of immigrants,

always has been, always will be – is accepted by most people, I would suggest, simply for the sake of a quiet life. And it is reflected in the language too. The use of the word 'indigenous' has virtually disappeared, to be replaced by far hazier (and more politically correct) phrases such as 'the traditional population' or 'the settled population'. If even these strike you as offensively monocultural in their connotations, then there is the option of 'people already here', a formulation I have come across during conversations with apologists for mass immigration and multiculturalism. Along with making Britain sound rather like a massive airport terminal, it abolishes at a stroke the idea of a nation in any meaningful sense, as a place with a developed set of traditions, customs and collective history.

Les Huguenots! Or the numbers game...

During such conversations and debates, the example of the French Huguenots is pressed into service with a regularity which has become as monotonous as it is predictable. The Huguenots, who fled to England in the sixteenth and seventeenth centuries to escape religious persecution, are just one of the 'waves' of immigration which, according to the new history of Britain, have formed the country and prove that we are indeed a nation of immigrants.

It has been estimated that during that period – which spans decades – between 50,000 and 60,000 Huguenots settled in England. Such a small number meant that the newcomers had little choice but to assimilate, and assimilate they did. Similarly, around 150,000 Jews from Eastern Europe and

Russia are estimated to have settled in Britain in the years between 1880 and 1914 (out of a massive total of three million who left those countries, mostly going to America). And by far the biggest stream of immigration into Britain pre-twentieth century was from Ireland, in the decades which came after the 1848 potato famine: in 1861 there was an estimated 600,000 Irish expatriates in Britain.

That there has always been some immigration into Britain is therefore not in doubt. Indeed, nobody has ever questioned it. But the amounts such as those quoted above, taking place as they did over centuries, are very small, both absolutely and in comparison with other countries, and certainly do not amount to evidence that Britain is the sum total of its migrants. As David Conway writes in his 2007 pamphlet 'A Nation of Immigrants?', from the early sixteenth century right down to the Second World War, very little of Britain's net increase in population can be attributed to immigration. He quotes J. A. Tannahill, who in his 1958 study European Volunteer Workers in Britain, observed:

> Britain is not by tradition a country of immigration. In fact, between 1815 and 1914, she not only quadrupled her population without resorting to large-scale foreign immigration, but also despatched over 20 million people to destinations beyond Europe, at first largely to the USA and later in ever increasing proportion to the developing countries of the Commonwealth.

For nearly 1,000 years, the stable nature of this country's demographic profile meant that all those factors which go towards making an identity, a culture, could develop and refine themselves: customs, laws, procedures, beliefs, values. That these were up until very recently, in historical terms, taken for granted and broadly agreed upon, is evidenced by the fact that there was never any pressing need to have urgent debates about British identity of the kind that increasingly dominate our own times. These 'national conversations' rarely get very far, largely because the terms on which they are held are set by people who have little basic sympathy with the very notion of the 'nation', and have mostly lost confidence in the defining qualities or uniqueness of this one in particular. The result has usually been that British values are defined vaguely as 'tolerance' or 'compassion' – qualities that would doubtless be claimed for themselves by most societies on earth.

So why has it been deemed necessary to recast Britain as a nation of immigrants? Quite simply, it is an attempt to make more acceptable to a deeply concerned population the unprecedented levels of immigration of the past twenty years, and thwart any opposition that arises from its understandable anxiety on seeing the rapid transformation of many parts of the country. Since the abandonment of any meaningful restrictions on immigration by the Labour governments of 1997 to 2010, the numbers coming to Britain have been staggering. According to figures from the Office of National Statistics, in the decade to 2004, migration into the country increased from 314,000 in 1994 to 582,000 in 2004, with most of the increase due to inflows taking place after 1997. Despite the various promises from the new coalition government that action would be taken to bring such figures down, they have in fact continued at the same level. It has been estimated that the British population is expected to hit the 70 million mark in just sixteen years' time (in 2028), with two-thirds of the increase coming from immigration; that's five million, or five times the current population of Birmingham.

The immigration which has taken place during this time, and its long-term demographic effects, will probably be seen by the historians of the future as the single most significant development to have happened in Britain in the late twentieth and early twenty-first centuries. It continues to be at the top of the list of most people's concerns. It has been shown by an all-party parliamentary committee to be of marginal if not non-existent economic benefit. The burden it has put on public services, especially during recessionary times, is heavy.

And yet, the political class appears still to lack the will to confront the issue. Or rather, it is scared of it. This might also account for the length of time it took for at least some of its members to finally admit that the ideology Britain had adopted in response to large-scale immigration – the doctrine of multiculturalism – had been a mistake.

The world within one country

Of all European countries, Britain was most zealous in taking the multicultural route in the second half of the twentieth century. In essence it was a doctrine which preached that all cultures were of equal value, that they should be encouraged to keep all their traditions and customs and that there should be no judgement passed, regardless of how much those traditions and customs might conflict with those of the host country. There was no question that when in Rome, one should maybe do as the Romans do; this was deemed imperialistic, arrogant and of course, racist.

Eventually the doctrine of multiculturalism found its way into virtually every corner of official Britain and by the 1980s it was firmly entrenched, its basic tenets accepted right across the political spectrum. Its high-water mark was perhaps reached during the New Labour years, when Lord Parekh came up with an influential report which called for Britain to become a 'community of communities'. In other words, we would cease to be a cohesive nation in any recognisable sense, but simply a federation of different ethnic and religious groups.

In reality multiculturalism meant that nobody should have to 'sign up' to any overarching sense of national identity, or system of values, although of course a lot of lip service was given to the desirability of this. But in every practical sense, official policy allowed for the maintenance of separate identities and communities, and, indeed, effectively encouraged it. Everything, right down to the use of multiple languages on local government forms, seemed designed to perpetuate difference and separation.

Long before the serious contradictions in this approach became clear and acknowledged, multiculturalism was enforced with a rigour which, to many people, seemed to go beyond the simple desire that people of different ethnicities, cultures and religions should all live in peace within the space of one (very small) country. If that had been the motive, then it could be called, at best, intensely naive but well-meaning.

But while there were undoubtedly some people who were driven, like the kids in the old Coke ad, by a desire to teach the world to sing and furnish it with love, the overriding dynamic behind multiculturalism was far more negative; it was to implicitly and explicitly attack the majority culture. For while multiculturalists made much of the need to rejoice in every aspect of every different culture, there was one glaring omission from the To Celebrate list: British culture.

Why was this? Put simply, it was never intended that British culture should be celebrated. Multiculturalism in reality meant that this or that group should be celebrated *in opposition* to the mainstream society. For behind this approach was a dislike of the whole idea of nationality, and a self-loathing distaste for British nationality in particular. Occasionally the cat would be let out of the bag by those on the Left, and in surprisingly crude ways – ways which did not shy away from using race in a way that no centre-right figure would dare. In one notorious example, Greg Dyke, when director-general of the BBC, complained of the corporation being 'hideously white'. Hideously?

The sheer weight of guilt felt by the liberal elites, which we explored earlier on, also meant that the adoption of multiculturalism was completely natural for them. It was an expression of their own preferences, their own self-hatred. It was as if they were saying: Don't worry about trying to fit in. We're terrible, after all, and you don't want to be like us. Our history? Don't concern yourself, for we are ashamed of it and just want it to go away too. We are the oppressors of the world, and we are responsible for all the bad things that have befallen you. You should realise that you are our victims, of course, and we are sorry, and rest assured, we will never, ever criticise you, nor hold you responsible for anything you do, ever again.

Obstacles to be overcome

Those who voiced concerns about where all of this might lead us were dealt with ruthlessly. The late Ray Honeyford, a Yorkshire headmaster of a school with 95 per cent Pakistani or Bangladeshi pupils, a public-spirited man and a great believer in the importance of education in fostering social cohesion, was relentlessly vilified, labelled a racist and forced to resign after he had written an article in 1984 in which he expressed the importance of learning English for children from different ethnic backgrounds. He questioned too the wisdom of allowing children to be taken out of school for long periods for visits back to Pakistan, a practice at that time defended as being part of their culture. He also voiced his belief that Muslim girls should be educated to the same standard as everybody else.

Honeyford was concerned about the divisions that were fermenting within British society. But his views were considered intolerable. The campaign against him, which included death threats to both him and his family, ensured that he was never allowed to teach again.

Now, at a time of increased concern about the toxic effects of multiculturalism, Honeyford's views have been accepted by the mainstream, if not actually acted upon. It is no longer considered an act of racist imperialism to say that immigrants should learn English; a politician who suggested it would not, perhaps, immediately have to tender his resignation. Yet echoes of this attitude persist: when it is announced that London is home to 150 different languages, or that within just a few years Birmingham will be Britain's first majority ethnic city, it is done with an air of celebration, as though something bad is being overcome.

There have been other casualties too of the drive for diversity at all costs. Chief amongst these has been the white working class, which has been so demonised over the past fifteen years that it is fair to say it is the only group in society now of which it is perfectly acceptable to mouth prejudice. Much has been written recently about 'chavs', and the apparent transformation of a people once regarded affectionately as the salt of the earth into something nearer to the scum of the earth. While left-wing writers cling to the notion that this was all the fault of Margaret Thatcher, others have put forward a more nuanced analysis, which tends to the view that in order to work, multiculturalism needed some sort of common enemy. The working class fitted the bill.

It helped that the political Left had grown exhausted waiting for the proletariat to rise up, and so had shifted their attention onto the more newly arrived, global victims of capitalism and white imperialism. Furthermore, the white working class, it was assumed, mostly by those who considered themselves to have impeccable liberal credentials, could naturally be relied upon to be thoroughly racist, intolerant and nationalistic, and thus the natural opposition to be fought. The fact that most of them were none of these things but were, understandably, starting to feel that they were being taken for fools, was neither here nor there. It became quite acceptable, especially amongst middle-class metropolitan media types (and I know whereof I speak), to complain about an area being 'very white', the implication being that such a place would be downmarket, provincial and not part of the vibrant, dynamic, diverse melting pot that was to be preferred (although of course, multiculturalism in practice provided *anything but* a melting pot).

What *would* we do without our nannies and gardeners?
This kind of attitude could be detected in an article, written in London's *Evening Standard* in 2009, which went on to achieve some notoriety. Andrew Neather, a former speechwriter for the Labour government, described – with obvious approval – the motivations behind government immigration policy. He had written a speech given by the then immigration minister in 2000 which had called for the loosening of controls, and which in turn had been based on an internal Cabinet report. This report had concentrated on the labour market, but as Neather went on to say in his article:

> … the earlier drafts I saw also included a driving political purpose: that mass immigration was the way that the Government was going to make the UK truly multicultural. … I remember coming away from some discussions with the clear sense that the policy was intended – even if this wasn't

its main purpose – to rub the Right's nose in diversity and render their arguments out of date.

Neather's article extolled the virtues of mass immigration into the capital, and he presumably expected his readers to be in agreement with him and not especially shocked by what he revealed. On this front, he misjudged the mood. But what was equally interesting was the attitude it displayed towards the working class:

> The results [of immigration] in London and especially for middle-class Londoners, have been highly positive. It's not simply a question of foreign nannies, cleaners and gardeners – although frankly it's hard to see how the capital could function without them… Their place certainly wouldn't be taken by unemployed BNP voters from Barking or Burnley – fascist au pair, anyone?

In other words, the only kind of white working-class person the writer could imagine was some knuckle-dragging neo-Nazi. And this from a *Labour* adviser.

Whether or not the nose of the Right was being rubbed hard enough in diversity, it was also during this time that more and more reservations about multiculturalism were being aired, and from sometimes unexpected points on the political spectrum. For example, David Goodhart, then the editor of the broadly centre-left magazine *Prospect*, wrote of his concerns over the effects that mass immigration was having on the traditional model of the welfare state. But it was the intervention of Trevor Phillips, as head of the Commission for Racial Equality, which probably had most impact. Anxious that the UK was becoming more and more divided on racial and religious grounds, Phillips spoke of his fear that Britain would become ghettoised along American lines. 'We are sleepwalking our way to segregation,' he said.

The fact that such things were being said by members of the liberal establishment was welcomed as proof that a proper debate was opening up. But after a few weeks of controversy, no meaningful discussion was really forthcoming. Multiculturalism might have been slipping out of favour, but it continued to cast a long shadow.

Shut up and celebrate!

The truth now was that many British people no longer knew not just what they could say, but what they could think.

This is hardly surprising, for even without being consciously aware of it, they have been caught in the middle of a contradiction. They are told to celebrate diversity, that diversity is a strength, that it is, in and of itself, a good thing, and that it should be the final aim of all political, social and cultural endeavours. But then at the very same time they are vehemently discouraged from actually observing differences in other cultures, or drawing attention to them, or even so much as acknowledging them. That, after all, runs the risk of earning one the ever-expanding label of racist. So, in other words, they must celebrate differences while at the same time pretending that there aren't any. It is like living within the pages of *Alice in Wonderland*.

It is understandable then that most people decide to retreat into silence. Either that, or talk endlessly about food and the extraordinary variety of restaurants their high street has to offer. Even now, with multiculturalism being seriously questioned and found wanting at every level, the array of cuisine remains the first thing to be mentioned by its apologists. It is no longer enough.

Research by the American sociologist Robert Putnam, the author of *Bowling Alone*, has suggested that diversity tends to affect levels of trust not just between different groups but, surprisingly, within each individual group. The greater the diversity, the greater the impact on trust. And there is another contradiction at the heart of the policy of diversity, explained by the journalist Christopher Caldwell in his courageous and thoughtful book, *Reflections on the Revolution in Europe: Can Europe Be the Same with Different People in it?*:

> If diversity 'enriched' and 'strengthened' nations as much as everyone claimed, why would any nation ever want its immigrants to integrate into the broader society? That would be *drawing down* the nation's valuable fund of diversity... Or was the supply of diversity meant to remain – via immigration – permanently on tap? No European public wanted that. So European leaders defended large-scale immigration in one breath by saying it would make their countries different (through diversity), and in the next by saying it would leave them the same (through integration).

Despite it being an implicit, wholesale repudiation of what for years has been promoted, integration is indeed the buzzword now. Quite how to switch to integration, when for decades you have been effectively encouraging people to remain separate, is a problem of such magnitude it should concentrate the minds of the whole political class. Is it even possible, while immigration levels remain so high? Any healthy society should be able to assimilate new people, and Britain has been more liberal and welcoming than many. Integrating 10,000 new people should not, over time, prove difficult; between 250,000 and 500,000 *a year* is a different matter entirely.

Such numbers mean that, other than the practical problems, there is simply little need or incentive for many immigrants to assimilate. Their culture will be all around them, intact and untouched. This is the situation as it exists for Britain today. Its leaders undertook a massive social experiment, unprecedented in modern history, and told nobody.

A nation of emigrants

The current government has stated its aim as being to bring down net migration to the 'tens of thousands'. This is something of a political sleight of hand, for it still takes little account of the size of the numbers involved. Half a million coming in and half a million leaving would, in fact, equal zero net migration. It would also surely mean that Britain had become little more than a floating landing strip.

During the years since 2000, emigration has been rising markedly; in 2004, for example, 350,000 people left Britain.

The profile of those going has been getting younger. The most recent figures have shown a slight reduction, which has been put down to the effects of recession. But the general picture over the past decade is of the movement of people on a huge scale, and a concomitant changing in the nature of the British population.

The same has been happening in London, the place which has elevated the principle of diversity to almost fetishistic levels, and whose increasing disconnection with the rest of Britain is held up as something to recommend it. It is a city which, according to the relentlessly promoted official view, is so wonderfully dynamic, vibrant and diverse, so obviously the best place known to man in which to live, that it's a mystery why anybody would want to leave. But leaving they have been: two million between 1994 and 2003. As with national emigration, the reasons put forward by those who research the matter are as hazy as those quoted by the people leaving, but it seems clear that there is some sort of white flight taking place. But a veil is drawn over this, as George Walden pointed out in his book *Time to Emigrate?*:

You won't find out from the press. They write about people moving out of London, but a disingenuous puzzlement infects their investigations. Vast numbers of people quitting the capital? Whatever can be happening? Could it be the stress of city life? The crowded streets and underperforming schools? Or is it the price of houses, the sense of insecurity, or simply the exorbitant cost of living? Or perhaps it's the call of nature, as the yuppies of yesteryear throw up their city bonuses and head

back to the plough? No mention is made of the ethnic compo-
sition of the leavers, so you could be forgiven for thinking
that black Londoners are tiring of life in Haringey or Brixton
and setting up smallholdings in Wales, or that Asians have
exhausted the pleasures of Shepherd's Bush and are taking to
the open road in search of space and solitude.

In 2005 I wrote about the area I had grown up in – Woolwich
in south-east London – in an article for the *Sunday Times*.
Traditionally a largely white working-class area, it had always
had a significant immigrant population which had been
accepted without a second thought. But over a few decades,
intensive waves of immigration had transformed it into a
fully multicultural town, and with it had gone any overarching sense of identity. Instead, I observed different groups and
cultures just existing side by side, uneasily and 'always with a
sense of nothingness in the air'. The whites left were either
the poorest of young families or pensioners. It was hard,
with the sheer number of different languages being spoken on
the train journeys in and out, not to feel alienated by the growing unfamiliarity of it. Perhaps it is this sense of rapid change,
this sense of displacement, which is at the root of the steady
exodus from London, and indeed from Britain as a whole.

Trouble in paradise

The reaction to my article, by the way, was interesting. It leapt
out at some people and I was duly asked to appear on various media outlets. I took part in a radio debate on whether
London was indeed becoming ghettoised, held in front of

an audience. Before going on air, the moderator thanked me for participating, as is customary in these situations, before adding that he thought what I'd written was a load of rubbish, but that it should be heard. I suspect that this was meant to show his broad-mindedness, but it was clear that my voice was considered peripheral to mainstream opinion.

The ensuing debate threw up some interesting questions and statements. The reaction of the audience, which was a pretty mixed one of whites, blacks and Asians, was nothing like as critical of me as the moderator had been expecting. There was indeed an obvious growing concern, amongst all groups, which was not reflected by the coalition of representatives on the panel, who generally attempted to paint a sunny picture. And something said by a white teacher in the East End, leapt out at me with some vividness: in an attempt, possibly, to ingratiate himself with the audience, he claimed approvingly that the situation at his (presumably predominantly ethnic school) had improved markedly since the whites had gradually moved away.

It would be hard not to see such a statement as racist if said about any other ethnic group. Why then would it pass uncommented upon here? This must surely be because the narrative of racism was that it was essentially something visited solely by whites on all other groups, who were themselves innocent and incapable of it. This is a belief which has been internalised by the liberal sections of the media, the evidence of which can be seen in the way that, for example, racist crimes perpetrated by whites are highlighted, while those committed by non-whites are downplayed, if reported at all.

It must have come as a shock therefore for many dedicated multiculturalists when it gradually became clear that there was prejudice and conflict between the different non-white ethnic groups. This was not, after all, what was expected. Darcus Howe, the veteran black broadcaster and activist, presented a television documentary in which he reported with alarm on the increasing tensions and indeed violence between West Indians and Somalis in Woolwich and neighbouring Plumstead, and West Indians and Pakistanis in the Midlands. In the programme a 16-year-old West Indian told how he was set upon by a large group of Somalis who caused near-fatal damage to his skull. 'When I talk about them it makes me want to be sick,' the boy said. 'I think they are vermin. They are not a civilised people. They are black but a different kind of black. To me they are like dirt. We have to clean up the dirt.' The programme also depicted Pakistani youths in Walsall threatening Mr Howe and talking about 'bashing' and 'mashing' blacks and Jews.

This kind of language would have resulted in a national outcry if used by whites about any other group. In this context, what it showed was that the last thing we seemed to have was a fully consensual melting pot. And in various parts of Britain, the uncomfortable fact was beginning to emerge that whole communities were living effectively separate lives, geographically together yet completely apart from each other.

Death in paradise

When the capital was attacked by four Muslim suicide-bombers on 7 July 2005, resulting in the deaths of fifty-two people, much was made of the steadfastness of Londoners in the face of the worst terrorist attack since the bad days of the IRA at its height. The media talked of the Blitz spirit, and how Londoners had come together, broken but unbowed.

But to many who were in London at that time, the atmosphere seemed somewhat different. There was bewilderment, and some anger certainly. But it was also possible to detect a sort of odd indifference. Many people seemed to have little real idea of what had just hit them, or why. It was the fragmented response of a fragmented city.

There was also undisguised shock from some quarters that the bombers were British born and bred, and that this attack had come from within. A video message made by the ringleader, Mohammad Sidique Khan, revealed him to be speaking in a broad Yorkshire accent. Here was somebody who had on the face of it been perfectly well integrated into the society around him, having attended Leeds Metropolitan University and been working as a 'mentor' at a local primary school. He was not the product of poverty, or badly educated, two of the clichéd reasons often trotted out to explain extremism. He was, as we would have been informed firmly by any multiculturalist before the bombing took place, as British as you or me.

However, what was most depressing about the long-term reaction to this attack – and indeed to the thwarted attempts at similar outrages which came later, again from British Islamist extremists – was the way in which initial anger was quite quickly converted into concern over possible so-called 'Islamophobia'. Whatever the views of ordinary Britons towards those who perpetrated London's 7/7 bombings, some commentators reflected what appeared to be an attitude of self-blame amongst large sections of the elites. Events – and morality – were effectively turned upside down. This was perhaps something we had brought on ourselves. We were, by implication, to blame. The war in Iraq was held up as the obvious motivation; if we hadn't engaged in it, then there wouldn't have been the massacre of fifty-two innocent people.

So many, especially on the metropolitan left, spoke with forked tongues: of course nothing could excuse such an atrocity, they said, but perhaps Iraq could explain why it happened. This was, of course, half way to excusing it, or at the very least, helped to lessen the responsibility of the terrorists for their own actions. And even if Iraq had been the reason, the thought that one should, in a country like Britain, have disagreements with government policy without resorting to mass murder never seemed to enter the minds of the apologists.

The terrible irony of course was that it was Britain – that most avowedly multiculturalist of countries, the country which had gone further than any of its European neighbours in encouraging each culture to maintain its traditions unhampered, the country that had required the least from its new inhabitants – which had been the first to produce home-grown suicide bombers intent on killing as many of their fellow citizens as possible. This apparent paradox threw up so many uncomfortable questions that it was easier to leave both it and them hanging in the air; instead much of the country appeared to go into a trance of denial about the extent of the threat it now faced. This was confirmed when the soul-searching after 7/7 quickly gave way to an overriding concern that the Muslim community as a whole should not be 'demonised'. Much was made of the claim that Islam was (by implication, uniquely) 'a religion of peace'. The Labour government even went so far as to try to rebrand terrorism as 'anti-Islamic activity'. The truth is that there was no real demonisation forthcoming; other than a few small incidents, there was little evidence of a serious public backlash against Muslims in general.

That the majority of Britain's two million Muslims lived ordinary lives, and did not support the actions of these terrorists, was not, and still is not, in doubt. But concern that there were indeed many people now who, by virtue of their culture or religion, did not want to integrate into British society, started to increase. This was not helped when the results of various wide-ranging polls of Muslims found a very significant amount (around 40 per cent) in favour of Sharia law in Britain, and widespread attitudes which could at the very least be described as illiberal, and certainly not at one with the values of a Western liberal democracy.

It was hard too, for many ordinary British people, to stomach the supine response of the political class when it came to dealing with the Islamist elements operating within the UK. In the 1990s, extremist preachers within (and without) mosques had been tolerated because, crazy as it may seem to us now, the British authorities simply did not take them seriously. This approach was in some respects a product of an inability on the part of an apparently increasingly secular Britain to comprehend that religious fundamentalism could be such a driving force. This was a failure of imagination on a grand scale. Terrorism, when it came, had to be the product of poverty, or alienation: people surely couldn't have blown themselves up (and many others besides) out of a sense of political or religious hatred. But it wasn't; and they had.

I will survive

Did Britain, in the first years of the new century, still have the stomach to defend itself, its values and way of life, against those who sought either to transform or destroy them? On a visit to Denmark to give a speech, it was utterly depressing for me to hear from some of those attending that Britain, whom since the Second World War they'd looked to as a particular beacon in the fight against extremism, was considered 'finished'. Coming from an atmosphere of general cultural appeasement in the UK, it was for me a sobering and shaming message.

The Danes had only recently become the focus of a whipped-up, orchestrated worldwide campaign of Islamic anger following the publication of the set of cartoons of Mohammad; the British press had chosen not to reproduce them, covering their cowardice with excuses about safety. References to Mohammad had been cut from *Tamberlaine the Great* at the Barbican; Islamist protesters were allowed to preach death on the streets of the capital while those passers-by who objected were shuffled away by police. The weak genuflection by Britain's cultural and political establishment to the book burning, marches and fatwa that greeted the publication of Salman Rushdie's novel *Satanic Verses* twenty years earlier had set the template: we would bow down rather than give offence, even if it compromised our freedoms.

Indeed we seemed more concerned with the freedom of those who preached our own destruction. Most recently, the Islamic cleric Abu Qatada, wanted on terrorism charges in eight countries, was released from jail in Britain, where he and his large family have been living on benefits since 1993, after the European Court of Human Rights decided he could not be deported to Jordan as this might violate his right to a fair trial. This is somebody who has called for the slaughter of Jews, Americans and yes, British people, while happily pocketing around £500,000 in public money from British taxpayers. Widespread calls that the Court should simply be ignored and that this man be deported regardless continued, at the time of writing, to go unheeded by the government, which despite its fine words, resembled a rabbit caught in the headlights.

For some, the tentativeness of officialdom when it came to those who might be encouraging or fermenting terrorist activity while living off welfare bountifulness was evidence that Britain had suicidal tendencies. The author and commentator Douglas Murray puts it succinctly:

The point is this: no society that wanted to survive would behave like this. No country with any short-term (let alone long-range) survival instinct pays the very people who want to kill us... We have gone from believing we should be punished to encouraging people to punish us, and finally paying people to punish us... For anyone who hates themselves, Islam provides the most marvellous opportunity. And the Islamists would hasten to agree: 'So you think you have a shed-load of guilt to bear and that you are worthless and contemptible? Well, we think so too!'

Murray hoped that the wisdom of the crowd would in time replace the cravenness of the political class. Certainly, that cravenness comes right from the top: Rowan Williams, the Archbishop of Canterbury, famously caused an almost audible sigh of exasperated despair when he loftily declared in a speech that the establishment of some Sharia law in Britain was inevitable. In a BBC interview afterwards, he dug himself further in: the idea that 'there's one law for everybody … I think that's a bit of a danger'.

A danger? We have to allow that highly educated people with impeccable enunciation can still be very, very stupid, but even so the Archbishop's remarks, coming as they did from the very heart of the establishment, could not have been better calculated to further unbalance British cultural confidence. Such an intervention did not help at a time when the country's Christian foundations appeared to be under assault from all sides (as well as from within). The only encouraging aspect to the affair was the obvious derision with which his observations were treated by the public.

Them and us, again

That same public would be forgiven for thinking that few of its elected representatives, or many of the great and the good for that matter, were fighting its corner. If anything there was the feeling that those above it regarded it as something which should be kept at bay by its, so to speak, elders and betters, many of whom had a distaste and indeed fear for what they imagined it thought.

So a very valid nervousness about those amongst us who wanted to harm us, and a suspicion that such people might perhaps number more than *bien pensant* opinion might like to admit, had to be characterised as unthinking Islamophobia. Bewilderment at the speed with which neighbourhoods were changing as a result of mass immigration had to be dismissed as small-minded and parochial. And as the real racial discrimination and prejudice of past times thankfully ebbed away, so the constant charges of racism, which have become such a feature of contemporary life, had to be ratcheted up and intensified.

All of this was badly to misread the vast majority of the British public. Indeed it was to do them a real injustice. They were portrayed as particularly xenophobic when in fact they had been more open to foreign influences then most other comparable societies (most restaurants in France and Italy are just that – French and Italian). They were talked of as particularly racist when in fact they were remarkably accepting, so long as new people paid their way and obeyed the law. They were dismissed as particularly insular even when they had shown every sign of giving multiculturalism the benefit of the doubt.

The sense that the country itself was negligent about the safety of its own people, that it cared more about the rights of an Abu Qatada than its own citizens, has certainly led some British people to, in turn, give up on the country. Who can blame them, when they hear, as they did in February 2012, that some 500,000 people have been allowed into Britain unchecked, opening up a serious breach in the country's defence against terrorists and criminals? How, they might ask, can one be proud of a society that seems to hold itself in such contempt, that seems so careless about its own wellbeing? Why then should *we* care? The answer might be that while it is unfortunately all too easy to understand such disaffection, it should be possible to be thoroughly ashamed of the incompetent actions, or inaction, of one's government without being ashamed of one's country.

Indefinitely British, definitely English?

In terms of British identity, the massive changes which have occurred over the past twenty years have resulted in developments which could not have been foreseen. While academics and policy wonks talked earnestly of a need to 'redefine Britishness' in the light of multiculturalism and demographic change, the atmosphere of dissection and deconstruction led to a surprising resurgence in a particular consciousness of Englishness.

This has been characterised by being almost solely from the grassroots. It certainly has had no official encouragement; St George's Day continues to be ignored. But a simple comparison between the crowds at the 1966 World Cup, and any international sporting event of the past fifteen years shows a remarkable change: in the former, we see a sea of Union flags, in the latter, a forest of St George's Crosses.

The English flag is now worn on sports clothing, flies from the bonnets of cars, and hangs out of the windows of semi-detached houses when England is playing. While researching an article on this extraordinary revival in my part of south London, I asked a wide cross section of people if and why they flew the flag. Most of it did indeed come down to sport; the flags duly disappeared as soon as England made its exit from whichever contest it was in (which was invariably sooner rather than later). But there were also touching and, especially from young people, unexpected comments which suggested that the flag was considered part and parcel of the country's identity; its symbolic function was not lost on them.

It has also become evident, even on a purely anecdotal level, that more and more people are reclassifying themselves as English rather than British. Certainly the growth in Scottish nationalism and an apparently unstoppable constitutional devolution have played a big part in this, as we shall see later on. And the federalising instincts of EU bureaucrats might also have had the (for them) undesired consequence of reigniting national identities.

But multiculturalism and mass immigration have been influential here too. If everybody can be British, then it follows that nobody is British – or rather, it can be viewed as an increasingly meaningless label. Calling themselves English is perhaps an attempt by many to save something, to hold onto something which appears to be at risk. That this might well be one of the chief reasons for the rise in English consciousness tends to be confirmed when one looks at the disdain with which it is viewed by so-called 'progressives'. Its ethnic connotations and its supposed lack of inclusiveness are anathema to them, as is the fact that in these islands, the English represent the majority.

The very vagueness of the modern use of 'British' continues to be, for *Guardian*-reading progressive opinion, its greatest virtue. Meanwhile, as the legal entity known as the United Kingdom prepared to celebrate the Diamond Jubilee of its Head of State, the political entity of Britain itself was in danger of becoming something even less than vague: it might cease to exist altogether.

CHAPTER FIVE

BREAKING UP?

In May 1977, to mark her Silver Jubilee, the Queen delivered an address to both houses of Parliament, gathered together under the magnificent hammer-beam roof of Westminster Hall. In a reign of otherwise impeccably non-political speeches, this one stood out in its apparent expression of a personal view.

The problems of progress, the complexities of modern administration, the feeling that metropolitan government is too remote from the lives of ordinary men and women, these among other things have helped to revive an awareness of historic national identities in these islands. They provide the background for the continuing and keen discussion of proposals for devolution to Scotland and Wales within the United Kingdom.

I number Kings and Queens of England and of Scotland, and Princes of Wales among my ancestors and so I can readily understand these aspirations. But I cannot forget that I was

crowned Queen of the United Kingdom of Great Britain and
Northern Ireland.

Perhaps this Jubilee is a time to remind ourselves of the
benefits which union has conferred, at home and in our
international dealings, on the inhabitants of all parts of this
United Kingdom.

Well, perhaps this Diamond Jubilee would be an even better
time to 'remind ourselves of the benefits which union has
conferred'. But it would now be impossible for the Queen to
make such a speech. Devolution, which thirty-five years ago
was still for many a vague notion, a debating point, is now a
fully fledged reality, a major political and constitutional issue,
and therefore one which rules out monarchical interventions
of any kind. How times change. And as she and her subjects
gave thanks for her sixty years on the throne, a question must
have been there, in the back of her mind. When James VI
of Scotland came down to London and became James I of
England in a Union of the Crowns, he effectively made his
illustrious predecessor Elizabeth I the last monarch solely of
England. Would she, Elizabeth II, be the last monarch of a
United Kingdom?

Alex Salmond, Scotland's First Minister and now established as one of the most recognisable political personalities
within the UK, has made it clear that a fully independent
Scotland would 'keep the Queen' as Head of State. In such a
situation she would, increasingly, be one of the few remaining
ties keeping the now separated countries together (she, and
a common coinage; Mr Salmond has mysteriously gone off

the idea of Scotland joining the Eurozone). But how long would even this tepid enthusiasm for a unifying monarchy last once she is gone? Back in 1977, when she toured Scotland as part of the Silver Jubilee celebrations, the cheering crowds had numbered in the hundreds of thousands. By the Golden Jubilee of 2002, they had dwindled to a fraction of that. It is far from guaranteed that an independent Scotland would welcome King Charles III with open arms.

Nice nationalism

'Being British' somewhat relies on there being a Britain in the first place. Many of us now exist in a state of confusion as to the country's very status as a legal entity. The historical amnesia which has afflicted our schools and academic institutions, which we discussed earlier, has ensured that huge numbers of people now know little about how their own country came into being.

Evidence of this could be seen in the celebrations in 2007 to mark the 300th anniversary of the Act of Union, i.e. there weren't any. The event passed largely unmarked and ignored, except by officialdom and the minting of a commemorative £2 coin. This was remarkable when one considers that, although England and Scotland had been joined under a single Crown in 1603, the 1707 Act formally created Great Britain, and a Parliament common to both countries. It was a hugely significant event. But people cannot celebrate what they do not know.

Furthermore, those who saw in the United Kingdom a modern triumph, a political union which was to go on to achieve great things and exert an enormous worldwide influence had been, ideologically speaking, rather on the back foot in the late twentieth century. In the 1960s and 1970s the political momentum had instead been with Scottish and for that matter Welsh nationalism, for amongst other things these represented an implicit attack on the status quo. It followed therefore that much of the support for these movements came broadly speaking from those on the political Left. Any form of nationalism, with its implied inwardness and aggressiveness, should, given their own internationalist and class-based politics, naturally be anathema to them. But Scottish nationalism was somehow considered the *right* kind. It was *progressive*. Such support was another example of the odd alliances and ideological somersaults the Left is capable of, on the principle that 'my enemy's enemy is my friend' (another example we were later to see was its alliance with radical Islam).

This wasn't the whole story of course. The gradual electoral extinction of the Tory party north of the border following the Thatcher era gave nationalism one of its chief dynamos, moving it on from its status as a political debating point to one as a front-burning issue. The establishment of the Scottish Assembly by the Blair government in 1999 was motivated, it was claimed, by a desire to actually strengthen the Union. If this were true, it was a serious error of judgement: Pandora's box was now well and truly open. In this context it is not difficult to see why Blair's successor Gordon Brown, MP for a Scottish constituency, made it such a personal mission to emphasise Britishness. The public was not convinced, and his (somewhat panicky) preoccupation with the issue came to nothing; indeed it is more than likely that he will prove to be the last Scots Prime minister of a United Kingdom.

Meanwhile, as he settles on a date for an Independence referendum (2014, the anniversary year of the Battle of Bannockburn, is his preferred choice), Alex Salmond's speeches and interviews are peppered with references to 'the people of Scotland' or 'the Scottish people'. The ascent of nationalist sentiment has meant that Scottish culture and history are talked of with unashamed, upbeat pride by those who are not even Scots, but who feel safe and, yes, politically correct in doing so. This is completely at one with the view that nationalistic feeling, when combined with a healthy sense of victimhood, is not just acceptable but positively hip.

The appearance of Mel Gibson's film *Braveheart*, which depicted in simplistic terms William Wallace's battles against the effete, tyrannical, despotic English, gave popular nationalism a remarkable boost, and briefly made Mel a hero there (a status which, in light of later events in his life, has probably been rescinded). Another movie star, Sean Connery, became a kind of patron saint of nationalism. Scottish faces might remain prominent on parliamentary front benches and across the London-based British media, causing the BBC's Jeremy Paxman to once complain of a 'Scottish Raj', but such an English presence, in Scotland, would not be tolerated. At its worst, some of the more virulent anti-English feeling north of the border would be condemned as racist if uttered by or about any other race or nationality.

Nasty nationalism

The growth in an English consciousness, which we looked at in the last chapter in the context of multiculturalism, was also undoubtedly a response to the rise of Scottish nationalism, the unbridled celebration of Scottishness which accompanied it, and the implied sense of criticism of England contained within it.

But the new, unformed and still incoherent feeling of a separate English identity, which started to make itself popularly felt during the 1990s, was not looked upon with understanding, much less endorsed, in anything like the same way as Scottish nationalism. This was a time, remember, of Cool Britannia, of metropolitan Europhilia, and a new start, a 'Year Zero' for Britain as a 'young country'. Indeed, Englishness was seen by *bien pensant* opinion and the political class as something to be resisted, not taken seriously, and as much as possible, ignored. The suspicion was that English nationalism was potentially dangerous; it was the traditional, aggressive and unacceptable sort. The English, after all, were not victims but oppressors. Nevertheless, movements for a separate English Parliament grew up, which, despite making no real political headway, proved tenacious, perhaps drawing strength from the conviction that their time would eventually come.

But there was another dimension to this: in the United Kingdom, and numbering around 45 million, the English represented the majority. It was quite logical for multiculturalists to continually emphasise Britishness, and to pour scorn on Englishness, for, as we discussed earlier, it appeared to them far less inclusive. And if one could talk as historians did of the 'tribes' of Britain, then the English were by far the biggest. They symbolised the political mainland from which others wanted to break away. They had also taken the overwhelming brunt of large-scale immigration, so their sense of themselves was, like Britishness, fair game for the deconstructionists. The comedian Eddie Izzard, for example, made one such attempt with his TV series *Mongrel Nation*. Nobody, surely, would dare tell the still largely monocultural Scotland that it was a mongrel nation. And no English politician would conceivably pepper his speeches with references to 'the people of England' or 'the English people'.

But much of the new English movement, if one can even call it that, came from a simple sense of unfairness. This had been bubbling away for some years, born of a feeling that both as a country and people they had been essentially hidden from view, kept under lock and key, a component which simply did not fit the contemporary picture. With the arrival of devolution red in tooth and claw, a popular feeling that they were no longer on a level playing field increased amongst the English. They became aware of what had been known and discussed by politicos for some time as the 'West Lothian Question': that Scottish Members of Parliament could vote on legislation which affected England, but that the arrangement was not reciprocal, with areas such as health and education in Scotland being strictly off-limits to Westminster. To the English, more and more seemed weighted against them.

Not just a question of money?
The resentment caused by the existence of such constitutional anomalies was compounded – perhaps superseded – by a feeling

amongst the English that the Scots received preferential treatment in other ways, most notably when it came to the public purse. The Treasury's Public Expenditure Statistics certainly seemed to bear this out, showing that the government's annual spending per person amounted to £10,212 in Scotland, compared to £8,588 in England.

A recent study by the Institute for Public Policy Research (IPPR) think tank and Edinburgh and Cardiff universities found that 45 per cent of voters in England thought that Scotland got 'more than its fair share of public spending', with 40 per cent believing England received 'less than its fair share'. Fifty-two per cent thought that Scotland's economy benefited more than England's from being in the Union. The number of those asked who thought that Scottish devolution had made the way Britain is governed worse had doubled since 2007 to 35 per cent and a massive 79 per cent also wanted to see a ban on Scottish MPs voting on English affairs.

All of this means that voters in England are putting more store by their specifically English, rather than their British, identity. Eight out of ten English voters were found to support what had become known as 'devolution-max' – the option which would give Scotland full fiscal autonomy, but would stop short of full independence. And nearly six out of ten did not trust the UK government to work in England's interests. 'There is strong evidence that English identity is becoming increasingly politicised,' said Richard Wyn Jones, professor of politics at Cardiff University. 'The more English a person feels the more likely they are to be dissatisfied with the way that the UK is being governed post-devolution.'

But along with this there is, too, a growing sense that the cultures of England and Scotland are going in different directions. Scotland appears more and more wedded to a liberal, social welfare mentality of the Scandinavian kind. England on the other hand, perhaps for the first time in decades, is seriously questioning not just the workings but the very assumptions behind such a model. Alex Salmond is a keen European; in England. Euroscepticism is on the march.

Whether or not all of this translates into a full-blooded desire in the English to break away, to become just England again for the first time in centuries is, however, doubtful. Resentment over the inequalities in the current arrangement might have markedly increased, as we have seen, but it would be difficult to assert that there was anything approaching real passion on the issue. It is perhaps easier to detect a mild, ongoing irritation with the apparently ever-complaining Scots, and a vague indifference about the long-term fate of the Union.

And the Scots themselves? The recent Assembly success of the nationalists in forming their first administration since devolution has perhaps obscured the fact that the desire to break away from Britain completely also remains relatively weak. With the real prospect of a referendum looming, polls showed that only a minority of Scots wanted complete independence: an Ipsos MORI survey carried out at the beginning of 2012 had the figures at 29 per cent for full independence, and 54 per cent for remaining within the UK. Amongst that 54 per cent was Douglas Alexander, the Labour shadow foreign secretary. As he vividly put it:

As a Scot, I have always believed that Scotland stands taller as part of the United Kingdom... The SNP declares that after independence Scots would become better neighbours and no longer surly lodgers. But the United Kingdom is a home we have built together and you can't be a lodger in your own home.

Our house

If we are indeed all under one roof, then perhaps it would be only fair that all family members should have a say in how the furniture is arranged. Independence is not something which happens in isolation. It takes two to break up, and in the case of the UK, there would be ramifications not just for England and Wales, but for Northern Ireland, which while not included in Great Britain is still part of the United Kingdom. Should not the English have a say in what happens?

In the certain absence of a similar referendum being held simultaneously in England on what would be the de-uniting of the United Kingdom, it is left up to those who believe in it to make the case to the Scots in the time remaining before they vote. In the *Daily Telegraph*, the columnist Charles Moore succinctly encapsulate the choice before us:

It could be that, like a marriage which was once successful but has now become acrimonious, our component nations should part. But we have done a great deal together... In what sense is the writing of Robert Louis Stevenson or Arthur Conan Doyle (both Scots) not part of the culture of the whole British nation? The 400th anniversary has just been celebrated of the

Bible translated on the orders of King James (the Sixth of Scotland, the First of England) after whom it is named. It forged and exported the most important common language and culture since that of ancient Rome. The United States, Canada, Australia, New Zealand and India are as they are in large part because of what the British did. The new £50 note records the partnership of Matthew Boulton, an entrepreneur from Birmingham, and James Watt, an inventor from Glasgow, who between them produced the steam engines that transformed the industry of the entire world. If you tear it in half, don't expect each bit to be worth £25.

It wasn't just the industrial revolution which witnessed and drew from the power of the Union. That England and Scotland are stronger together than apart had been demonstrated almost from the very moment the Act of Union was passed in 1707. For the next two centuries, the building and maintenance of the British Empire saw Scotland play a disproportionately large part; it has been estimated that one out of every three colonial governors after 1850 were Scots. 'What began as a hostile merger, would end in a full partnership in the most powerful going concern in the world ... it was one of the most astonishing transformations in European history,' said the historian Simon Schama in his 2001 television series, *A History of Britain*.

Perhaps though, that global success means little to diehard Scottish nationalists, who might in any case shrink at the sound of imperial trumpets. Their pride is an exclusively Scottish one. But given the magnitude of the possible change at hand, those on the other side of the argument, who should be pointing out what we would be throwing away, have so far shown themselves to be lacklustre. Certainly, David Cameron, speaking in Edinburgh, did describe the richness of the shared culture, naming those famous Scottish figures, from Adam Smith and David Hume to Walter Scott and Lord Reith and declaring that 'your heroes are our heroes'. He also said that while he was proud to be English, he was proud to be British too, and that he was a Unionist heart and soul, saying 'I am ready to fight for my country's life'. All this is commendable, but there needs to be much, much more if nationalism is to remain a minority interest and the Kingdom United.

British or English pride?

The fact that the overwhelming numerical dominance of the English in the UK has inevitably lead them, over the years, to tend to think of 'English' and 'British' as interchangeable terms and identities, has also perhaps instilled a complacency missing in the other parts of the kingdom when it comes to the questions now presented by devolution. And it's not just the English who do this: most Americans I know will happily talk about how much they've enjoyed their trips to England when of course they mean Britain, sometimes in mixed company (not the kind of mistake to make when Scots are present).

Such jumbling up of identities is inevitable, and shouldn't be used as an excuse to separate them even further. We all of us, historian or hack, do it all the time. Nobody really means to exclude the Scottish or the Welsh when they describe (as they increasingly don't) the ideal of the 'English Gentleman'. Others might talk of the marvellous English countryside as a source of their pride, and in the same breath mention as examples the magnificent Highlands or Welsh mountains. 'The Queen of England' still slips off the tongue more naturally somehow than the awkward-sounding 'Queen of Britain,' but we will then refer without a second thought to the *British* sense of humour, or the *British* use of irony.

English Literature will include of course the study of Scottish, Irish and Welsh writers, and although this is drawn from its basis as English as a language, it doesn't stop the English themselves on occasion claiming Oscar Wilde, Conan Doyle or Dylan Thomas as part of their tradition. But then we talk almost exclusively of *British* theatre and *British* cinema (our ballet, on the other hand, tends always to be English). Great eccentrics are celebrated still as being an English rather than a British breed (for no good reason) whereas that famous fondness for the underdog, and its flip-side the suspicion of success, is described (quite accurately) as interchangeably a British and an English characteristic. And although we talk of the *British* stiff upper lip and *English* reserve, the acts of 'muddling through' and just 'getting on with it' were, in the past at least, regularly admired as belonging to both.

The Act of Union was already a century old when, at 11.45 am on 21 October 1805, at the beginning of the Battle of Trafalgar, Admiral Horatio Nelson ordered the running up of his famous flag signal to his men: 'England expects that every man will do his duty.' It remains even now, in our educationally challenged times, one of the most famous lines from our history. But it was Britain that was at war; the men serving under Nelson were in the British Royal Navy. HMS *Victory* was a British ship in a fleet which included Scottish, Welsh and Irish contingents. Now of course, we would do anything to avoid damaged sensibilities and the taking of disgruntled offence, but it's to be imagined that Nelson's men knew what he meant.

The English, Scots and Welsh have, as British soldiers, fought side by side in countless battles since then. What united them on such occasions must have seemed infinitely greater than what divided them. At the most serious of moments, the British tend to become unequivocally just that. There has never been any muddling or mixing when it comes to describing the events of 1940, when for a crucial time the country stood alone against Nazi Germany. It was, and always would be, the Battle of Britain, and Britain's finest hour.

CHAPTER SIX

WHAT ARE WE LIKE?

When the newly created Duke and Duchess of Cambridge appeared on the balcony of Buckingham Palace after their wedding, both they and the hundreds of thousands gathered below were treated to the customary fly-past, which on this occasion included a Spitfire, a Hurricane and the last remaining flying Lancaster bomber. It was a moving and rousing sight. Later on that day, I took part in a discussion about the wedding and the monarchy on an American radio station. *The Guardian* journalist and broadcaster Jonathan Freedland was a fellow guest, asked on to proffer the republican perspective. He pointed out that there had been no need at all for the planes of the Second World War to be there, but that their inclusion was part of an attempt by the monarchy to marry itself to the strong 'creation myth' of modern Britain, one which centred around its wartime experience, and especially, the memory of Britain in 1940, fighting alone against the Nazis.

Of course, the fact that the Prince is in the RAF was probably a very good reason for the planes to make an appearance, but no matter. I was relieved that Freedland did at least point out that yes, this creation myth was based on fact, i.e. we really were standing alone. For, as we discussed earlier, in the decades since that war, the British have become used to a gradual yet relentless chipping away at their history, their achievements, their great men and woman, their very sense of themselves. They have been encouraged to believe that what appeared to be fact was probably illusionary.

The same goes for national characteristics, customs and ways of behaving: historians and social commentators line up to tell us that no, the British were in fact never really like this, or yes, 'twas ever thus. Sometimes you get the impression that they are trying to reassure themselves, rather than us, when faced with some alarming new development or frightening event which they cannot readily explain. The riots of summer 2011 are a case in point: don't get too worried, we were told, for this was part of a British tradition – compared to past examples, this was a tea party, etc. Just relax.

Anxiety about change and decay – and it is widespread now, and certainly not just amongst older generations – can be too readily written off as misplaced nostalgia, or a wilful desire to see the worst. Worried and scared by increasing anti-social behaviour? Don't be alarmist – didn't you know Britishness has always had a thuggish element? Dismayed by the loss of our customs and traditions? You need to adapt!

Concerned about the debasement of the language? Don't be silly, it's vibrant and just evolving.

But people live with the evidence of their own eyes all around them, every day, and it is difficult for them not to feel that the character of the British has changed, sometimes, it would seem, out of all recognition.

Once caricatured as excessively reserved and buttoned up, we now seem to be strangers to emotional restraint. Instead, we seem to cry buckets at the drop of a hat – or at least, on being told we have not made it into the final line-up of *The X Factor*. Our once much-mocked embarrassment at showing feeling has given way to an uninhibited desire to spill our guts out on TV talk shows. Similarly, our often-remarked-upon sense of civility and collective decorum has given way to the scrum. The courtesy once so remarked upon by visitors has vanished as though it were never there. A culture which, for better or worse, had a horror of personal embarrassment now barely understands the concept of shame, as anyone who has witnessed the fall-out from an evening of mass drinking in any one of our city centres can attest to. And what was once a keen awareness of the privacy of others has mutated into a pride in ostentatiously not giving a damn.

But like clichés, stereotypes tend to hang around, and usually have more than just a sliver of truth in them. So at this point it is perhaps worth looking in some detail at just a few of the more famous characteristics and customs associated with the British – our public behaviour, our sense of fair play, our pragmatism, our humour and our infamous class system – and explore the extent of the transformation.

The queue: on its last legs?

Queuing (or, as you can increasingly hear it referred to in London, standing-in-line) is still evoked by foreign journalists trying to get a grip on the British as one of the best examples of the national mentality. Its basic unimpeachable fairness is an expression of social cohesion. It relies on a strong sense of communal feeling, and an assumption that those around you share the same outlook. It has that essential 'gentleness' that George Orwell wrote about when he described the national character. And on more occasions than not, it is a completely voluntary practice.

With these considerations in mind, it becomes very easy to see why it is a custom which appears to be on its way to extinction, certainly in the main urban areas. Much of modern Britain has no time for or awareness of such nuances. They simply don't 'do' queues. The bus stop queue is the most obvious and common sort, and it is here that the change is most stark. Anybody on their travels around London will not have to look far to see that once orderly lines have been replaced by crowds who mill about, waiting for the bus to arrive, with no sense of precedence, no awareness that those waiting the longest should be first on. When the time comes to mount, there is a sort of slow-motion free-for-all. Few people show any anger about this. Perhaps it is impossible to get worked up about queue-jumpers when there is no queue to jump.

It is very easy to mock a preoccupation with something

as small-time in the scheme of things as the humble queue. But in such details can one detect the drift of a society, and the death of the queue, though gradual, has come about in a remarkably short space of time. Its demise is not total; interestingly, it is in what one might refer to as 'privatised' areas such as banks and supermarkets that it still thrives, but that is because it is rigorously enforced and is not strictly speaking voluntary. In the public realm, such as on transport, it now doesn't stand much of a chance.

What happened? Some might suggest that Britain is now home to many people for whom queuing is an unfamiliar practice. But I don't agree; in my experience many newcomers have shown surprise at the lack of order in a country where they had expected it. No, I think that perhaps many British people – let's hope not the majority – are now simply too selfish to queue. By its very nature, queuing requires the putting of somebody before yourself. It also requires that at some level, in the past, you would have to have absorbed a set of values which gave such an act meaning. In large parts of our society, such values are no longer even transmitted from one generation to the next, so it could be argued that younger people especially are not to be blamed for not knowing. If a child is not even taught that it should respect its teacher at school and do what it is told, as is now so often the case, it can hardly be expected to act in a civil way towards others in the wider public sphere.

It's not just kids of course. Our society has become oddly snobbish about such customs as queuing. It places people in a context which suggests perhaps too strongly for many of them that they are simply one of many. It makes them feel silly. In a modern culture which increasingly encourages people at every juncture to consider themselves uniquely special, regardless of talent or deed, such an act of submission to the wider public good is a gesture too far.

The strain on the train

The same kind of attitude – of complete indifference or outright hostility to others – can be seen around us every day. On my return to this country after five years in the USA, I was immediately struck by the change in the public behaviour of many of the British. The contrast with America, which contrary to some popular prejudice, is a remarkably courteous and civic-minded place, was vivid. I am not talking here about outright anti-social behaviour of the kind that required the now defunct ASBOs or gets headlines in the *Daily Mail*, but rather the low-level, everyday stuff: the way people treat each other in the public arena – in trains, restaurants and on high streets.

I've written about this on a number of occasions and for one such article spent a week going about my usual business, commuting and working like millions of others, but with one difference: I decided to speak up on those frequent occasions which cause many of us minor stress, every day, to see what happened. People speaking loudly on phones, swearing at the tops of their voices in crowded trains, putting their dirty shoes up on seats – all those sorts of alienating bits of behaviour which degrade most people's daily routine, were part of my brief. Friends thought I was being either brave or foolhardy – a reaction which itself shows how far the situation had gone.

I was not knifed, which was a relief. But overall the reaction of those I approached (as politely and beseechingly as possible) showed that a fundamental shift had occurred. It was I who was considered the trouble-maker, the rude one. People were aghast at being asked not to mouth off four-letter words when there were tiny kids present. Many looked surprised and angry when asked to, please, keep the phone conversation down a bit. Requests to consider that somebody would have to sit on the seat where dirty shoes now rested were met with derisive smirks or sometimes verbal abuse. Few people offered me any support when it might have been most appreciated, although they usually voiced it to me quietly afterwards.

There are still some romantic souls around who see the suffering in silence of most people in the face of such behaviour as being typically British. Nothing, they say almost cheerfully, is more characteristic than our desire not to make a fuss. This is a nice, reassuring interpretation but unfortunately it is out of date. People now don't challenge even such seemingly superficial examples of anti-social behaviour because they are simply frightened of doing so. They don't want to get physical or verbal abuse and they have made the calculation that it is a risk not worth taking.

Unfortunately, in a world in which a father can get beaten unconscious for asking a gang not to swear in front of his small children, that calculation is the right one.

At one time complaining about uncivil behaviour would have made one ripe for mockery as one of *Private Eye*'s

Bufton Tuftons or a Disgusted of Tunbridge Wells. But concern about the rapid coarsening of our public life, and all the alienating nastiness that flows from it, is no longer the preserve of tweed-clad retired majors, but emanates from all parts of the political spectrum and across all generations. The 2011 riots, with their aimless, nihilistic destructiveness were in many respects an extreme continuation of the low-level anti-social behaviour which we had, without thinking, become used to – something which was tacitly accepted even by many liberal commentators who, unusually for them, found them-selves on this occasion lost for words.

Trash and burn

As ever, for the Left it was Mrs Thatcher who was to blame for these changes, along with global financial meltdown, harsh winters and the decline in Cher's singing career. They have fixated on her famous (but misquoted) statement that 'there is no such thing as society', as emblematic of policies which praised and elevated the individual and in so doing undermined any wider collective sense and tore asunder the very fabric of the nation.

But whatever one's attitude to Thatcher, the emphasis on a sense of individual commercial enterprise, and the belief that the individual should take responsibility for his or her own actions, do not (and did not) lead inevitably to social break-down on the scale that Britain now faces. Such a situation takes a lot, lot longer to come to the boil. Rather, the roots of 'Broken Britain' lie in the wholesale dismantling of authority in all its forms, whether legal, social, familial or moral, which has taken place over the past five decades, the trashing of institutions, and the long-term, insidious effects of a counter-cultural emphasis on the gratification of individual desires at whatever cost (an attitude that is about as far from Thatcher's own value system as it's possible to be).

For the so-called New Left of the 1960s, and their massed contingents of naive out-riders, authority in whatever form had to be opposed on principle, as did any established custom regardless of how efficient or benign it might be in practice. We are still living with the effects of this, and indeed, with the people: the generation who grew up in the 1960s and 1970s are now running much of the show. The institutions and beliefs that gave both internal and external structure to people's lives – especially, working-class lives – were attacked and hollowed out. Religion, patriotism, a collective sense of national identity, the belief that our institutions were essentially on our side, all these things were systematically discredited.

Alongside this, the belief grew that any form of restraint, official or just personal, was destructive to 'personal fulfilment' and wrong on principle. The less serious members of the new countercultural movement happily went along with this as a sort of joy ride, the chance to cock a snook at traditional rules and ways of doing things while having a lot of fun along the way. The more politically motivated, fed up with waiting for the (obviously reluctant) proletariat to rise up according to the set plan, saw a chance to deconstruct the traditional culture from within.

We have come a long way from the time when it was

considered inconceivable to answer back to your teacher. A very long way, right to the point where tentative and disarmed policemen stand back and watch as rioters smash windows and loot shops. But the progression is a completely logical one. Indeed the change in attitude to the police is instructive.

It is easy to be too sentimental about the bobbies of the past, and the fatherliness of such TV figures as *Dixon of Dock Green*, but there was nevertheless a strong element of truth behind this picture. The traditional British attitude to its police was always markedly different to that in most European countries, where they tended (and still do) to be more coldly regarded as enforcers of a law handed down from above. Here, as with the Common Law from which our legal system arose, they were seen more as being on the side of the ordinary man or woman in the street; in fact they had mostly come from the same kind of communities they policed. The middle-class professionalisation of the police force (or 'service' as it now likes to refer to itself), its obsession with political correctness in the aftermath of the hugely damaging Macpherson Report, and a sense amongst the public that its chief aim is no longer simply to protect them, has meant that the old attitude has largely disappeared, never to return.

The British wobbly lower lip

Restraint, rather than Cyril Connolly's famous pram in the hallway, is now seen as the enemy of individual promise in Britain. Most forms of it have taken a battering, and this includes the personal, emotional variety. Britain's attitude to displays of feeling has flipped since the days when Celia

Johnson and Trevor Howard kept the turmoil strictly below the surface in *Brief Encounter*. With its twittering accents and dominating sense of social decorum, David Lean's classic film is now, for many, hard to watch with a straight face. It is extraordinary to think that in its time, it would have certainly resonated with the audience. The past is not so much a different country as an alien planet.

Few now argue that a woman should stay in a tedious marriage for the sake of husband and children. But, when one pays close attention once again to that film, now well over half a century old, it is hard not to be moved by its nuances and overwhelmingly adult sensibility. Many have the sneaking sense too that in the years since, we might have gained an incomparable level of choice, but in the process lost something else.

We are encouraged not to 'bottle up' our feelings and to share our innermost thoughts. The emotional incontinence of this new touchy-feely Britain had its most famous expression in the days after the death of Diana, Princess of Wales in 1997. Coincidentally, it happened only a few months after the election victory of New Labour, and the promise of a 'new' kind of Britain. Many people looking on at that time, at the weeping and wailing, the shrines and the teddy bears, had the sensation that they were living in a different country to the one in which they'd grown up. The public reaction was proof to many that the British 'stiff upper lip' was finally obsolete, and it was hard not to agree. Just as witnessing tears in another can make one well up too, so the orgy of grief seemed to gain its own momentum.

Looking back at those days, one starts to feel a mild embarrassment. What the hell was going on? Shock must have played a part. That the princess was particularly popular is not in doubt. But people seemed to be crying more for themselves in some way. They were caught up in the drama of it all, and as the grief became the story, so were they firmly at the centre of it. They had become the national equivalent of those little knots of weeping schoolgirls who gather round the now ubiquitous roadside shrines, all claiming to have been the deceased's best friend; the emotions are skin deep, and as is quite natural for the very young, tend to dissipate as quickly as they came. If this seems harsh, then it's worth considering how quickly the apparently apocalyptic sadness displayed over Diana faded. But it did leave us with questions about ourselves. Did the whole episode show, as some suggested, that in losing its hang-ups, Britain had 'matured' emotionally?

Yes – if your idea of maturity is a self-centred and self-pitying belief that what you feel should be automatically displayed regardless of the context. The truth is that this is exactly how a child behaves. Far from growing up, many of us had grown down. And sure enough, in the days since Diana's death, tears have flowed with ever-decreasing discrimination in public and on television, and the effect has been to degrade and coarsen our emotional responses. A quick look at archive footage of the crowds at the funeral of Winston Churchill in 1965 will show the silent, mournful and respectful faces of people both young and old, and from all backgrounds. But they are not tear-stained; and their sadness appears all the more genuine for it.

Those who glory in the wobbliness of the British lower lip make the big mistake of equating emotional restraint with coldness. To which one should say that the deeper and more felt the emotion, the harder it might be to express.

The C-word

There is the view that the stiff upper lip was essentially a middle and upper-middle class characteristic, one that characterised the world of Celia and Trevor, and which was also displayed to morale-boosting effect in other films of that period, such as *In Which We Serve*, in which Noël Coward did a fine, buttoned-up imitation of Lord Mountbatten, stoical as Captain of the torpedoed HMS *Kelly*.

But this is too restrictive. It might have been manifested in different ways, but the 'keep buggering on' ethos was common to more than just solid Home Counties types and admirals. It could be seen in working-class people in a kind of dogged persistence, a belief that you just kept going on because, frankly, what else could you do? There was no point in sitting around moaning and whining. But when it is mocked and satirised now, it tends still to be in the context of Empire and the class that built and administered it.

It's something of a minor achievement surely to have come this far in a book on Britishness before considering class as an issue. This is after all traditionally meant to be one of our chief obsessions, along with the weather, and certainly it is constantly being redefined and re-examined for signs of contemporary relevance. At the time of writing, another television series on the subject is airing on the BBC. But class in Britain has radically changed. In the past the obsession around it centred on accent, tastes, clothes and all sorts of other external indicators. Whether or not you were 'U' or 'non-U' according to Nancy Mitford's famous code – whether or not you said lavatory or toilet – was what mattered to many. The socially aspirant had numerous sources to go to for guidance, many of which were only half tongue-in-cheek. *The Official Sloane Ranger Handbook*, published in 1982, was just as much a style bible for wannabes as it was a humorous send-up of so-called Hooray Henrys.

But this kind of class obsession has, I'd suggest, faded to the dusty periphery in contemporary Britain, if not disappeared entirely, which must be a good thing. As was mentioned much earlier on, the early 1980s saw a final fling, a muted purple blast, of a certain kind of retro interest in all things aristocratic. An aesthetic born of the country house had certainly set the benchmark for what was considered good and bad in home decorating: basically, new was bad. Michael Heseltine could be talked of disdainfully by his snootier Cabinet colleagues as the kind of man 'who has to buy his own furniture'. No matter how successful one had become, it was possible to be 'kept in one's place' simply by being labelled nouveau riche. It resulted too in what might be a uniquely British kind of self-reinvention – the person from humbler origins who went out of their way to acquire the manner and style of their so-called betters. It's possible to argue that the self-transformations wrought by a Noël Coward or an Edward Heath would not be taken seriously in modern Britain, and neither would they be necessary.

But even if this approach to matters of class long ago lost any sway it had, it would be wrong to assume that economically defined class has disappeared. Far from it. What has changed is the shape of the class structure, our attitude to it, and who we see as being 'above' and 'below' us in the scheme of things. We now resemble more of an American model, where financial success, or simple fame, are the great guarantors of status. Indeed the term 'nouveau riche' has fallen into disuse. For many younger people now, who use the newly revived term 'posh' to define the successful and rich, there is no difference between Victoria Beckham and Princess Anne.

At the same time, it would appear that the middle class has swelled and swelled and burst its banks. This is particularly true if one includes in the definition of middle class any work which does not include manual labour – which, increasingly in Britain, is a niche activity. Of course it is certainly possible to argue that one can be doing 'clean' work, at a desk staring at a computer all day long, and still be, in real economic terms, working class. But what you consider yourself to be is all-important, and even though people continually label themselves working class when asked by pollsters, it is more than likely that they are giving the answer they think is most acceptable. Underneath, they probably think of themselves as straight-up middle class.

Move on up?

Britain and class might have been joined together like a horse and carriage in the minds of others, but the truth is that even in the past, ours was a more fluid society than many others, with less of the petty social distinctions and snobberies that exist in supposedly more egalitarian European countries (France springs to mind here). Nevertheless, the past decade has seen the re-emergence of certain, quite particular kinds of snobbery in Britain, which have developed not from some sense of social standing, but from where one stands in relation to the political and social orthodoxies of the day. The politically correct so-called yummy mummy who lives in a whirl of neurotic activity would be aghast at being called a snob, but in her attitude to the Essex girls down the road, and in her much-trumpeted preference for organic food, she is just that. Impeccably liberal she may be, but she detests what she assumes are the views and priorities of her affluent but flashy neighbours. The still-unvarnished vowels that display quite recent working-class origins prove to her that they probably hold views she'd find reprehensible. They probably don't pay enough attention to global warming. And the fact that they have the occasional McDonald's puts them beyond the pale.

Recent years have also seen social mobility between classes, which was increasing in the decades up to the 1980s, come to a grinding halt. This is one of the most worrying aspects of life in Britain today. It is statistically verifiable, but one can easily see it on a day-to-day level too. For example, the industry I have spent much time working in, the media, used to be considered quite classless in a modern way, booming and expanding as it did after the 1960s. Now, however, most of the people I meet in it I can expect to be privately educated. The same is true of journalism, which used to be one of the traditional routes out of the provinces for bright young state-educated people. The professions have once again become the province of the public school educated. And on a purely social level, there is less and less mixing between classes, although this is obscured by the superficial similarities of dress, speech and leisure pursuits.

Supporters of the grammar school system point out that the drastic decline in social mobility came about as a direct result of its abolition. Certainly the timing of both makes this a convincing argument. These schools (of which a few remain, the object of intense competition amongst parents) were an exceptionally effective way for clever, ambitious kids to move from one set of career expectations to another. But their disappearance is not the sole reason for the current situation. The carnage that has been wrought by so-called progressive methods in the wider state education system – the wholesale junking of discipline, coupled with the mantra of child-centric self-expression at any cost – has left generations of ordinary kids betrayed and marooned. Britain's slide down the international educational rankings has been truly shameful: we are now ranked at twenty-fifth for reading and twenty-eighth for maths. The obsession with social engineering and a crushing culture of mediocrity has left state school kids chronically unprepared and ill-equipped in the face of a battalion of public school leavers honed on a diet of high aspiration and self-discipline. Increasingly, they do not stand a chance when faced with the big wide world.

The emergence of an almost Hogarthian underclass, of people of minimal education who are not only unemployed but realistically unemployable, and whose lives are characterised by the absence of context or external meaning, is one of the features of British life in the past fifteen years. This has been widely commented on as a social problem with no apparent solution. What is less commented on, however, is the more general decline in the belief in the value of education as a good in and of itself, and as a means to 'moving up'. Surveys have shown that when asked, an alarmingly high percentage of children will state their aim in life as being the desire to be a 'celebrity'. This, and the loss of faith in working hard to achieve success, are both examples of the slump in the perceived value of deferred gratification. Sacrificing today for something better in the future is a notion which is increasingly just read about within the covers of old novels. It might be the new model of a car, or personal status and recognition: people want it, believe they deserve it, and they want it now.

I'm ordinary, get me out of here!

The cult of celebrity, the end of which is regularly trumpeted but which never seems quite to happen, has certainly had an impact on how many people of school age in Britain view themselves and their prospects. As the perplexed older Thatcher, played by Meryl Streep, says in the Oscar-winning film *The Iron Lady*: 'Back then, we wanted to *do* things. Now people want to *be* somebody.'

What is striking about the current obsession not just with stars of film, television and music, but with an increasing band of personalities of no discernible talent or distinction, is that the hold it has in Britain is so completely at odds with what we thought was the traditional British character. This country should have been the last place one would hitherto have expected there to be such a complete embrace of every aspect of the cult: the hype, the celebration of fame as a quality in itself, and the slavish attention given to the personalities who populate all positions on the celebrity spectrum, all run counter to our supposed dour cynicism about such things. The obsession with the doings of TV stars is in fact greater in Britain even than in the supposed home of modern celebrity, America, and is concentrated too on the tackier end of the market.

This is part and parcel of the decline in a no-nonsense approach to life which until recently ran through so much of British culture, from everyday routines through to the way in which we governed ourselves. It has been there in our constitutional development, and is most strongly in evidence in a popular resistance to political ideologies of any hue. In this, we stand quite apart from most European countries. It is not to say that there hasn't been a strong radical tradition in Britain. From the Levellers to the Chartists to the early days of the Labour movement, there have been organised, sometimes revolutionary challenges to the status quo founded on strong principles, convictions and a way of looking at the world. But change in Britain, whether or not it has been brought about by these movements, has always tended towards the incremental, with bloodshed relatively absent.

It would sometimes take a period away from Britain to fully appreciate its basic pragmatism and strongly developed sense of what was real and what was fraudulent. 'Typical!', 'I'll believe that when I see it', or the now more or less extinct

'Come off it!' were all expressions of a wariness about the extent of human possibilities, a resistance to showiness and a suspiciousness towards great schemes or ideas. Of course it had its negative aspects, the most grinding of all being a distrust of success and an excessive fatalism. But many of us would rather live with this downside than with the present culture of self-aggrandisement, fame-worship and an addiction to conspicuous display paid for on credit.

Are we the fairest of them all?

One result of British pragmatism was that instead of ideologically inspired aspirations to *egalité et fraternité*, there existed the belief that one should strive for fairness in life's arrangements. Quoting a sense of fair play as a famous British trait might make the cynical roll their eyes; it conjures up comical chinless wonders complaining that something's 'not quite cricket, old chap'. But a belief in fairness as a characteristic of a decent and civilised society was there, entrenched, in the back of our collective memory, and informed the way we judged more aspects of life than we even realised.

Needless to say, this has taken one hell of a kicking in recent years. The parliamentary expenses scandal exposed many MPs to be liars and cheats, some on a grand scale, others petty (it's difficult to know which is worse) and damaged the reputation of Parliament to such an extent that it is now hard to envisage circumstances in which it might recover to its former levels. The British have always had a healthy disdain for politicians, but underlying the cynicism was also the feeling that they were probably decent (if misguided) people who had the country's best interests at heart. Certainly, people could take an understated pride in the fact that compared to the majority of the world's governments, ours was untainted by corruption. That belief was hugely shaken by the scandal.

At the same time, the shamelessness of many in the financial sector, and the colossal salaries and monstrous bonuses which were then justified on the flimsiest of grounds, turned a distrust of banks and other financial institutions into smouldering contempt. The sense that here were people creaming off the rest of us became widespread. The sight of executives being paid stratospheric amounts even after having proved utter failures, symbolised by the case of the former boss of the Royal Bank of Scotland (ex) Sir Fred Goodwin, was offensive to basic instincts of decency. Add to this the revelation that parts of the press had been systematically hacking into the phones of private individuals, and had worked hand-in-glove with the police, and you were left with a situation in which confidence in our institutions had hit rock bottom.

Of course, many on the political Left took great delight in all this. Interestingly, however, they received virtually no political dividends from the crises. Demonstrating students might swing from the Cenotaph, and anti-capitalists might set up tent cities, and both might enjoy great media attention, but there was no radical surge from the broad sweep of the population. Perhaps this was because, while they felt angry and betrayed, they were equally preoccupied with another form of unfairness, one which struck right at the heart of the very concept and which they could see on their own doorsteps: the increasing and widespread abuse of the welfare system.

The very point of the welfare state was, at its best, based on fairness: individuals in a community put in, and in turn took out when the need arose. It relied on a strong communal sense, and a solid social cohesiveness. But these were not the circumstances as they existed in Britain in 2012. In the decade or so up to then, the penny had finally dropped for most people that welfare was paid for by their taxes, not from some magic tree only the government had access to, and that there were untold numbers of people who choose to live off the public purse, having made the calculation that working wasn't worth it. Outright fraud was widespread. Government research found that the majority of those claiming 'incapacity' benefit were in fact able to work. The political argument over the proposed capping of benefits at £26,000 – an amount out of reach to millions who worked for a living – served to increase the sense of injustice. And the reality of thousands of new arrivals to Britain, and their families, having access to the same level of free care on the National Health Service as those who had paid into the system all their lives, seemed to many to be the very definition of unfairness.

An atmosphere in which they appeared surrounded by people on the take – on the TV news, in the papers, at the local job centre – certainly started to rub off on the British. A recent study of 2,000 people by the University of Essex found that standards of personal honesty, as measured by an 'integrity' meter, had declined drastically within the past decade alone. And it was also not so surprising that a poll carried out by *Prospect* magazine in 2012 found that a massive 74 per cent of people thought that Britain spent too much on welfare and should cut benefits. They did not disagree with the principle of welfare, which they saw as consistent with British values, but felt that the wrong people were benefiting. People did not need the *Daily Mail* to tell them this; they could see it all around them every day.

Celebrating the ancient British custom of trick or treat

What they also see around them are little changes, little disappearances which make the place more homogenised, less obviously familiar. This is the point at which the nostalgia buffs amongst you sit up and take notice. However, one really doesn't have to have such a long memory to get wistful, for so many of the small incidentals that were traditionally part of British culture have disappeared or been transformed in very recent times. The blame for this – if it's something which you consider requires blame – can be placed not at the door of incoming cultures, but rather on a decline in the British sense of themselves.

When recently living at Shooters Hill, one of the highest points in London, I would watch the celebrations for Diwali, which take place in November, in that part of the East End of which our windows afforded a stunning panoramic view. Thousands of little explosions, all beautifully controlled it seemed, and by their size obviously emanating from hundreds of back gardens. Then a few weeks later would come Guy Fawkes Night – or rather Guy Fawkes week, as the random setting off of rockets and golden showers seemed to start earlier and earlier and end only when exhaustion set in. There was no rhyme or reason to any of it. Instead the spirit behind it all seemed to be one of aggression. It had increasingly become yet another opportunity to go a bit wild.

There might still be grand firework displays on 5 November, but fewer and fewer people now have much of an idea what they are meant to be marking. Certainly kids no longer ask for a penny for the Guy; these little stuffed effigies have disappeared into the pages of reference books about lost British customs. And in their place have come bands of gaudily dressed kids demanding sweets and money with menaces.

Hallowe'en, USA-style, is now big business, with all the major supermarkets offering every conceivable accessory for the perfect celebration. There's a lot of money to be made here, but that's not the sole reason for the explosion in popularity of this particular festival over the past decade. Rather, it is because those same kids are now more familiar with the rituals of suburban America than they are with those of their own culture. Many of them would have had holidays in Florida; most of them would have seen *ET* and its charming Hallowe'en scene. Nothing wrong with either of those of course. But the ease with which one custom has faded and another quite arbitrarily taken up is testament to the weak grip our own past traditions now have on many British imaginations.

We're, like, so into that now?

Furthermore American and even Australian popular culture have become the sources of information on how to behave and speak not just for British teenagers but for parents determined to appear indistinguishable from their offspring. The excruciating upward verbal inflection, which transforms every sentence into a question, came to our shores with the daytime soap *Neighbours* and took up permanent residence. It is now pretty much universal in Britain. Similarly, after ten years of *Friends*, we increasingly ask to 'get' a cappuccino 'to go'. A form of low-rent American management-speak has colonised our conversation off duty as well as on. Schools organise 'prom nights'. We increasingly 'mail' things. We talk about what happened 'back in the day'. When angry, we now 'flip the bird' or 'give the finger', the British two-finger salute having almost completely disappeared within the space of a single generation. And in certain urban areas in particular, a form of Jamaican dialect – so-called 'Jafaiken' – has become the speech to be aspired to amongst young whites. Indeed this is not just a matter of the odd inflection; it has been taken up wholesale, producing sometimes frankly surreal results.

Should any of this matter? Perhaps not, if you agree with the language experts that this just shows the dynamism and, yes, vibrancy of our ever-evolving language. But is it not also possible to detect an element of unconscious rejection in it? That the widespread adoption of quirks and ticks from another culture are an expression of a desire not to be of this place? Perhaps 'the other' offers more excitement. Or perhaps it is just that the familiar has become so weak it no longer transmits itself.

Certainly what we could call the 'up-ness' inherent in these newly acquired speech patterns offers little room for understatement. They are more naturally attuned to hyperbole and self-dramatisation. The British were, at one time, known as masters of understatement; it could be used to both devastating and comic effect. But much of the way in which we express ourselves now runs completely counter to it: TV audiences whoop, whistle and cheer with as much abandon and lack of discrimination as their American counterparts. Excitement has to be generated at every opportunity in such circumstances. And the need to now 'talk up', to hype, exaggerate and excite, can be heard in everyday conversations.

Are we having a laugh?

Their knack for understatement was at one time something which even the British found funny about themselves. This and a kind of end-of-the-pier campness, a naughty-but-nice vulgarity, were big components in popular British humour. Both of these have more or less disappeared, or if they are attempted now, it is either with a crudeness which goes against that original spirit, or a strong air of self-consciousness.

In 2011 *Prospect* magazine asked on its front-cover the question, 'Is British Humour Dead?' The broad conclusion it came to was that it was alive and kicking. But the fact that the question was asked at all was interesting. After all, we're living during a time when comedians play whole stadiums, and when the serious dissection of comedy as an art form fills page after page of the broadsheet culture sections. Comedy and comedians have always been with us but now they are treated as fashionable in the way pop stars once were. It is a golden era, it seems, for British humour.

Why then, despite the sell-out stadiums, the plethora of TV and radio panel shows, and the omnipresence of big comic names in the media, does it sometimes seem that there is so little to laugh at? Perhaps it is the wrong question. Perhaps the right question to be asking is why does it seem that there is so little to laugh at *together*.

British television sitcoms, from *Till Death Us Do Part* and *Dad's Army* to *Porridge* and *Only Fools and Horses*, achieved enormous audiences and devoted followings within the country. The shows of *Morecambe & Wise* were watched regularly by upwards of 20 million viewers – the kind of figures which current comedians can only dream of. Performers such as Frankie Howerd and Les Dawson became genuinely beloved national figures. And the satirical, more middle-class end of the market, such as was featured in programmes like *That Was the Week That Was*, enjoyed an influence and retrospective affection which it is hard to see any similar format replicating today.

Of course technology has played a big part in this – audiences have fragmented as channels have proliferated. But a truly popular star, or series, can still transcend this (as we have seen with the success of the drama series *Downtown Abbey*). Rather, it is the fragmentation of British society itself which could be the reason for the absence of collective laughter.

Of all forms of entertainment, comedy most requires a set of shared assumptions and values. We see in the comedian a representative of ourselves, up there on the stage perhaps, but somebody nevertheless who is essentially laughing with us, at our own foibles and our collective, cultural ones too. An air of familiarity is crucial to the most popular comedy. This is something which becomes harder and harder to sustain in a country such as Britain which has chosen a multicultural path, and which then seeks to celebrate all of those different cultures individually. Shared assumptions not only cannot be made, but would be actively discouraged on the grounds of insensitivity. It is difficult to explain the decline of the sitcom, for example, in any other way.

Many of the most modish comedians now are, like their forerunners, observational in style. But the palette they use is a narrower one. Moreover much of their material is streaked through with what can only be described as cruelty: they are laughing *at* rather than *with* (the TV series *Little Britain*, which enjoyed a brief but intense burst of popularity, is a perfect example of this). This is not to say that their audiences don't realise this. You get the sense that many of them are laughing heartily on principle, to show that they are onside with the prejudices or hobbyhorses of that particular comedian. They are in the cool gang. In this respect they really are reacting like the fans of a new and 'edgy' rock star. And as with the rock star, the comedian can then fall out of favour very quickly, with his devoted but now bored followers denying that they ever liked him very much anyway (Ricky Gervais being a good example of this), and complaining, in true rock-speak, of how he has 'sold out'.

The decline in a sense of social embarrassment and in the traditional nuances of class differences have also taken much of the steam out of British humour. From *Pygmalion* down to *Keeping Up Appearances*, it often relied on the comic potential of saying or doing the wrong thing in polite company, or being a fish out of water (as Del Boy declared while at a posh do in *Only Fools and Horses*: 'There we are Rodney! The crème de menthe of British society!') And undoubtedly, some comedy was increasingly seen as simply unacceptable. Certainly, there were faces which had been regularly on television for years but which, by the end of the 1980s, had completely disappeared.

Have you heard the one about Obama?

Interestingly, much of the comedy that disappeared was of the traditional working-class variety, which with its uninhibited use of stereotypes was simply too rich for the blood of the TV executives of the time. There's no question that much of it strikes us now as crude, certainly when it comes to matters of sex and race. But in its place came an approach which was equally monolithic.

Modern British comedy, born as it was in the so-called alternative movement of the 1980s, is a very middle-class affair. That is not to suggest that it is polite and conventional, far from it. Rather, it has taken its cue from the political and social sensibility of the university common room and the student union. Racism and sexism or anything that smacks of them are out, but there are a whole host of other taboos unflinchingly observed by our politically correct comedy establishment. A joke at the expense of the environmentalist movement, or mockery of multiculturalism, is never heard. You will almost certainly never hear a gag about Islam (unless it comes from a Muslim) for then, of course, there could be real consequences for our supposedly cutting-edge comics. Tories might remain fair game, just as in the days when spitting out the word 'Thatcher!' or 'Bush!' was a quick way to get a cheap laugh. But it's unlikely that a joke mocking President Obama, even after four years in office and a legacy of disappointment, has ever passed the lips of your average Radio 4 comedian.

British humour is splintered. Its different parts might be individually very popular, but it is something which is rarely experienced collectively now. When you survey the problems that face us as a country, this is indeed something to be regretted.

Sunlit uplands

No society can or should be preserved in aspic. Of course customs, habits and ways of looking at the world change; nobody visiting France would seriously expect to come across many stripe-shirted, beret-wearing cyclists with rows of onions slung around their necks. And undoubtedly the globalisation of travel has led to a general ironing out of cultures, a homogenisation that has left many societies feeling anxious about the perceived loss of their identities and cultural attributes. But having said that, the transformation in British society, as measured by the examples we've looked at, really does seem to be have been particularly revolutionary. According to some, this has made us happier, more relaxed, and, in that newly time-honoured phrase, comfortable in our own skin. Take a cursory glance around the current British landscape, however, and those three qualities are not the ones that immediately spring out at you. However, all is far from being lost. A more lingering look reveals some nice surprises and encouraging signs, which we will turn to next.

CHAPTER SEVEN

REASONS TO BE CHEERFUL

The possession of a sense of irony is something much prized by many British people, not just when it comes to humour but also for dealing with the slings and arrows of outrageous fortune. Americans tend to be condemned for not having a sufficiently developed one (unfairly, as anybody who watches *Curb Your Enthusiasm* can attest to) and the Europeans – well, even after all this time we still don't really know what makes them laugh.

Taking a thoroughly ironical approach to life can sprinkle a person with a sheen of sophistication. It's attractive and funny, but after a while, when the archness starts to wear thin, you can find yourself wanting something sincere, something meant, something which is given to you straight rather than coming from around a verbal corner. A sense of disappointment, even defeat, is implicit in irony, and most of us, while appreciating the cool cleverness, finally find ourselves hankering for something from the heart, some enthusiasm, some passion even. Indeed, some of us will even tolerate earnestness.

In the 1990s, Britain rather overdid the irony, or rather, its media did. We were living in 'Cool' Britannia after all, and everything that was promoted as good and worthwhile about the country at that time were also things which, paradoxically, you couldn't and shouldn't show much enthusiasm for without appearing, well, uncool. Design, fashion, Brit Art, Oasis – these were essentially the accessories to a metropolitan, ironic lifestyle, for people who wanted to live their own, mini-version of the Swinging Sixties. The so-called Generation X took to enjoying things their parents might have liked, such as *The Sound of Music* or prawn cocktail, but this time round, ironically. Comedy relied hugely on it.

But too much irony can start to feel like a living death. And if this was where Britain was to end up as the twentieth century drew to a close – endlessly self-referential, mocking itself to oblivion, an eyebrow constantly raised when looking at its image in the mirror – one could be forgiven for thinking that the game was up.

We're still here

But it wasn't. The cult of irony faded as new problems, unforeseen in Britain in the 1990s, such as Islamist terrorism had the effect of forcing down all those raised eyebrows. People found themselves having to consider who and what they believed in, and what they really thought about this issue and that value. Despite the obsession with celebrity and trivia, a strong strain of seriousness also started to make itself felt. And the efforts at 'rebranding' Britain, which had dominated the previous decade, were retrospectively regarded, as they had been by unfashionable commentators at the time, as plain embarrassing.

Patriotism and a pride in being British, in the sense in which most people still understood these things – that is, based on history, culture and institutions – had never been part of this 'modernisation'. But then neither had it figured in political or cultural preoccupations for the twenty, thirty or forty years before that.

Attempts at rebranding were in fact the least of it. As has been explored in this book, in the years since the Festival of Britain in 1951, the country had endured a massive cultural onslaught. A counterculture which was antipathetic to the whole idea of nation and national pride had exerted a far-reaching and malign impact on British national life. Partly as a consequence of this, but also because of liberal guilt on the part of the country's cultural establishment, the educational system had virtually ceased teaching the national story in any meaningful sense. British identity had been dissected and deconstructed in the face of multiculturalism, a doctrine which was followed to the letter to destructive effect, and which brooked no opposition. British culture was mocked and ridiculed. And 'regional' nationalism, defining itself in opposition to Britishness, threatened to take apart the actual political reality of the nation itself.

And yet.

Despite all this, and astonishingly perhaps to many, pride in Britain, as expressed by its people, has shown a quite remarkable capacity for survival.

Battered and assaulted from seemingly all sides, it has had every reason to keel over and die. But it remains, a testament perhaps to the ability of basic underlying values to withstand not just the vagaries of social fashion but outright political attack.

The strange survival of British patriotism

In 2011, Demos, a centre-left London think tank which had been closely associated with New Labour and its rebranding urges, carried out a survey on the state of British patriotism which it then put into a report entitled 'A Place for Pride'. The poll, based on a weighted cross section of the people of England, Scotland and Wales, and numbering over 2,000, delivered some startling results.

Chief amongst these was that a massive 79 per cent of those taking part declared that they were proud to be British citizens, a figure that would surprise surely even the most optimistic. The report revealed that pride in the nation was stronger in Britain than in any of the main European countries except Norway. Eighty-one per cent said they were 'proud of how Britain looks (e.g. its landscape, architecture and style)'. A further 74 per cent agreed with the statement 'I am proud of British culture' and 72 per cent declared themselves proud of British history.

When the participants were then asked about the extent to which they took pride in institutions and cultural icons as symbols of Britain, the results were equally revealing. The list is worth looking at in full:

Institution or cultural icon	Proportion of respondents taking pride
Shakespeare	75 per cent
The National Trust	72 per cent
The armed forces	72 per cent
The Union Jack	71 per cent
The pound	70 per cent
The NHS	69 per cent
The monarchy	68 per cent
The BBC	63 per cent
British sporting achievements	58 per cent
The Beatles	55 per cent
The legal system	51 per cent
Parliament	47 per cent

What is most vividly illustrated in this list is that the traditional symbols and institutions of the nation – including, as we can see, twentieth-century ones – are still seen by most people as sources of pride in contemporary Britain. The big majorities for flag, monarchy and armed forces could, one imagines, have been the result if the question had been asked in the 1950s. The popularity of Shakespeare and the National Trust as sources of pride should be enormously encouraging to those who fear that our cultural heritage is being lost in the mists of time. And 70 per cent viewing the pound as something to be proud of should be seen by all those reviled Eurosceptics as a heart-warming vindication.

The survey also found that while 41 per cent of respondents agreed with the statement that 'immigration contributes to British culture', 64 per cent believed that it can 'make it harder to identify "Britishness"'. With this in mind perhaps, a huge 78 per cent agreed that having a citizenship test for people to become a British citizen was a good idea, a figure which rose to 82 per cent when they were asked if such a test should include a 'values' element.

And, representing a riposte to those who immediately equate patriotism with incipient racism, the survey also found that those with greater levels of personal patriotism actually had less antipathy towards immigrants. Asked whether non-British people living in the UK were 'generally trustworthy', those who identified themselves as proud to be British citizens were almost twice as likely to agree as those who were ambivalent or negative about their own identity.

Fings ain't wot they used to be?

Nearly half of the people questioned also thought that Britain's best days were behind her. One might say that this is a recognition of an obvious fact, if you tend to the belief that the British Empire represented the zenith of Britain's achievements and influence in the world, although equally, if you don't, your optimism could spring from the view that Britain's resolutely un-imperial future represented something preferable to its past. But neither view is a bar to still feeling pride in your country and national identity.

What also emerged from the survey is that people felt that patriotism had declined over the past fifty years, with people being a lot less proud than past generations. Their own, present day professions of pride appear to show this to be untrue. But such a sentiment is not so surprising, when one considers the anti-patriotic onslaught the country has experienced during that same period. If the message you receive day in, day out from commentators, academics and intellectuals is that somehow such pride is wrong and harmful, that it is old hat, you too will start to believe that the days of being patriotic are, and should be, over.

The report which contained all these findings was a curious one. Choosing as its front cover tagline the quote 'Being British is more about doing your bit than things like Buckingham Palace', it seemed determined to come to the conclusion that Britain's attachment to the traditional symbols listed above was actually weak. This was flatly contradicted by the findings as we can see, so instead, it emphasised the results of those in the survey who had called themselves 'very proud' rather than 'proud' when asked the questions. Naturally, the corresponding percentages were much lower.

But this is a big mistake. Given the nature of this book, there would be no prizes for guessing correctly that I would call myself patriotic. Yet like most other people I can think of, I would not generally have called myself, if questioned by these pollsters, 'very proud'. It would just seem unnecessary to me; 'proud' should be enough.

The best of us

Pride in the armed forces came through loud and clear in the survey. However, an actual *increase* in the esteem in which they are held in modern Britain has been noticeable for some time.

In the past decade they were of course brought right to the fore of national life as the campaigns in Afghanistan and Iraq wore on. The increase in support for them can be seen at the anecdotal level. When the Princess of Wales's regiment left St John's Wood to relocate to Woolwich (my home town) in 2012, large crowds gathered to see them off and to welcome them at their new home. Parades of homecoming troops are similarly well-attended up and down the country. And when the recently formed Military Wives' Choir recorded a charity song, it went on to be one of Britain's fastest-selling singles.

But the renewed sense of respect in which they are now held also stems, I'd suggest, from the sense amongst many that together the armed forces make up one of the few institutions in Britain that actually appears to work as it should. Army, Air Force and Navy have been left untainted by the corruption and veniality discovered amongst those 'above' them, who are in charge of telling them where they will fight, and how much equipment they can expect.

And there is something else. The sight of resourceful, self-disciplined and yet invariably modest young men and women, all possessing a strong sense of duty, is both a relief and an antidote to the monopoly which the boorish, the self-absorbed and the thuggish seem to have on our attention much of the time. If these are the worst of us, then the soldiers are the best of us; and as the best, they take risks and possibly die on our behalf. The worst, meanwhile, steal trainers during a riot and post their triumphs on Facebook.

But does our support for the military tell us anything about patriotism and British identity? Yes, because the armed forces are inextricably linked to these very things. The point of them is to protect us as British people. Their allegiance is to the country as represented by the Crown, and not to politicians. It would in truth be difficult for somebody with little or no sense of national pride to cheer them on.

Lest We Forget

Another example of admiration for the forces is to be seen in the extraordinary growth in recent years in the observance of Remembrance, held every year on 11 November. The official ceremony at the Cenotaph in Whitehall, attended by government and royal family, and held on the Sunday nearest to Armistice Day, had been an unchanging fixture since after the First World War, and Remembrance poppies had always been worn by the public in the weeks leading up to it. In the 1970s and 1980s, protestations from the Left that it 'glorified war' became quite common, but as well as missing the point entirely, the criticisms went largely ignored. Now, other than complaints about 'poppy fascism' by Channel 4 newsreaders, such protests are rarely heard, and the marking of the actual day itself, in the form of a public silence, has increased. Similarly, the sales of poppies grow to greater levels with every year.

These things have been happening from the grassroots. Newspapers might then jump on the bandwagon, create awards and run campaigns, but their efforts would come to nothing if there were not already in place an increasing sense of identification with the armed forces.

And then there has been Wootton Bassett. This small Wiltshire town, with a population of around only 11,000, has become nationally famous in recent years for the quiet, dignified way it has paid its respects to the bodies of servicemen which have passed through it after having been repatriated to nearby RAF Lyneham. What started out as purely a local affair became bigger as people travelled from far and wide to stand as the flag-draped hearses drove by. In recognition of the way in which it had effectively spoken for the country, the town was granted the prefix 'Royal' in October 2011, the first time in over a hundred years that such an honour had been bestowed.

The tributes of Wootton Bassett are important to a discussion about Britishness in a number of other ways too. On those occasions, we saw British people behaving in a way that many of us thought had disappeared for good. There was no Diana-style thrashing and wailing on show, and the world of reality TV programmes seemed a million miles away. Instead there was a still and silent reserve. Many of those who had travelled to be there were putting other people – the dead, their relatives and friends – before themselves. And also they were paying respects to an idea, albeit unconsciously perhaps, and that was that in dying in the service of their country, these young men had done something noble and worthy of respect. That such qualities and ideas should be celebrated should give anybody who feels despair for the future of British identity grounds for considerable hope.

Head over heart

Talk of public service and duty brings us to the Queen. At the time of publication, the Diamond Jubilee celebrations of her sixty years on the throne will be reaching their climax. It is a golden rule for any writer never to take unnecessary hostages to fortune, but suffice it to say that as I write, it has just been announced that, with three months still to go, councils have already received some 3,500 applications from people wishing to hold street parties. My local pub, my work building and the small private school in which my sister works have also all got events in the pipeline, and these are the kind that do not require such applications.

At this stage in the run-up to a royal celebration, it is customary for there still to be considerable apathy and talk of flops and damp squibs. But it is different this time, certainly when compared to the Golden Jubilee of 2002. The desire to celebrate is manifestly there. If anything momentum appears to be with the jubilee rather than with the expensively and exhaustively hyped Olympics. There is a feeling that this is an occasion of real historical significance. Those who complain spuriously about such events encouraging jingoism and the like are conspicuous by their absence. The link between monarch and the expression of national identity is, on occasions like jubilees, an explicit one. Such events allow us to take stock of ourselves and how we have changed, and this one, celebrating as it does sixty years – the timescale roughly covered by this book – is a truly momentous one.

Moreover in the past decade, this monarch in particular has moved onto a different plane in terms of her status as Head of State and in the general respect in which she is held. Although sheer longevity alone plays a big part in this, her personal ethos and style – of low-key devotion to duty – is the main reason why the monarchy, which had been talked of as drifting towards the periphery of British life, has managed in the early twenty-first century to drift right back to the centre again.

As we discussed in the last chapter, the emotionalism symbolised by and surrounding Diana was used as a counterpoint, a modern alternative, to the supposed coldness, the buttoned-up emotional repression, of the Queen and the generation and class she represented. It was also an implicit attack on the 'old' Britain and its values of perseverance over self-expression at any cost. But time has a great way of sorting the wheat from chaff. If indeed there was a sort of battle for the self-image of Britain, symbolised crudely by the question 'Queen or Diana?' then it's fair to say it is now over and done with. The Queen won.

Flagging up our beliefs?

The picture we painted at the beginning of this book – of a country with such little sense of itself remaining that it seemed to be like a patient on life-support – would seem to be flatly contradicted by the findings in opinion surveys, the enthusiasm for the jubilee and the admiration and affection which is increasingly manifested towards our armed forces. Such high levels of pride in the country, its culture and symbols surely prove that actually, the patient has quite sound basic health.

But people, even if they are in the overwhelming majority, can feel pride in their country and yet still feel angry, sad or frustrated. They can – and do – feel that they live in an atmosphere which dictates that they *shouldn't* be proud, that they should apologise, that they are wrong-headed – or worse, that there is nothing to choose between them and a bunch of fascists or racists. It has been my intention to try to explain why this is.

Certainly, despite the fact that the majority of us tell pollsters that we are proud of being British, there is something almost covert now about expressing Britishness. For a long time patriotism has had an almost *subversive* feel about it (especially the newer, specifically English brand). We have it despite being told not to. Of course, there is no actual law against it, nobody telling us that to wave a flag is a criminal offence. But laws and edicts are not necessarily needed in such a situation. The dominance of a set of hostile attitudes and beliefs, which then proliferate like tentacles throughout our society and its institutions, can do the job quite nicely.

In fact attitudes to the flag itself provide a good example of this. We are told quite frequently by apparently concerned liberals and their right-minded fellow-travellers that far-right groups such as the BNP (and before them the National Front) have spoilt the Union flag for all of us. They have stolen it for their own use, have left it tainted and us ashamed, and understandably we have become very nervous about displaying it. Occasionally there are calls to 'take back' the Union flag, and more recently the St George's Cross, from the clutches of the extremists.

But where is the evidence for this? Do winning British athletes at the Olympics think twice about draping themselves in the flag for their lap of honour, for fear of being seen as BNP supporters? Do the Indian-run shops in my local high street discuss earnestly the risk they are taking before selling jubilee bunting, as they have already started to do? I don't think so. There is the flag, and then there is the BNP using the flag: telling the difference between them causes most people little trouble.

The truth is that those who tell us that extremists have hijacked the flag and made it unusable are not genuinely concerned about this 'problem' – *because they tend to think that fondness for the flag is extremist anyway*. Despite what they might say, they are not anxious to 'take it back' because they have an instinctive antipathy to such symbols. They are the ones who make an immediate connection in their minds between flags and bigotry, and then assume that others must too. It is rather similar to the old line about those with dirty minds seeing dirtiness in everything. And in a wonderful circular movement, they can then claim that because it has, as they say, been hijacked, anybody who displays or waves it must therefore be a rancid chauvinist with racist tendencies. Where that leaves people who have T-shirts, cushions, socks or anything else which the Union Jack now fashionably adorns, is anybody's business.

Are the times a-changing?

Alongside the findings of polls, buoyant belief in our cultural symbols, and public enthusiasm for national events, there are other, small changes which should also give us heart. There is, for example, a sense that people are feeling a little freer about voicing their concerns, in a way which simply wasn't the case even a few years ago. Certainly a wider, chronically overdue discussion on the effects of mass immigration on social cohesion and a coherent national identity is becoming patently unavoidable to everyone except those in a state of the most impenetrable denial.

What is also detectable is that those who have lived by the liberal-left political and social orthodoxies of the past forty years, and might have had some hand in imposing them, sense that they are losing their grip. Beliefs, indeed worldviews, which were accepted for decades as being gospel are being seriously challenged. The doctrine of multiculturalism, and the view that an ever closer integration with the EU was both inevitable and desirable, are just two examples mentioned in this book where years of received wisdom are being up-ended. But it goes further than this. Those people who have for years guided the values which inform public policy; who have decided what should be taught; who have set the terms on which welfare should be given; who make decisions about what we see and listen to: all these people feel the ground shifting uncomfortably beneath their feet.

The level of anxiety that undoubtedly exists about British identity, and the feeling that those who govern us and set the terms of debate in our culture have played a big part, in numerous way, in bringing about and fostering that anxiety, are, in a strange way, encouraging. If people really didn't care about these issues, then one might legitimately question whether there was much future for us as a cohesive, identifiable society. But the fact that concern is popularly felt, even if there are continual attempts by officialdom to douse it, should give us a form of reassurance.

CHAPTER EIGHT

LOOKING FORWARD

I f the British patient is indeed ailing, but has basically a firm constitution, how then do we get her fully back on her feet in this new century?

The gentle patriotism of old, often still so beloved of romantic conservatives and people living in the country, was a lovely ideal in many ways. It was polite and self-effacing, and had an almost majestic sense of melancholy of the sort to be found in the music of Elgar. It made much of rolling green hills, the presence of God in the details, and a belief that our success in the world came from the fact that much as we might like them and their more passionate ways, the peoples of other countries simply didn't have our sense of what was what. It relied on a notion that, unlike those who suffered from less self-assurance than us, we did not need to make a song and dance about who we were. We were not as *vulgar* as them. Of course implicit in all of this too, was a sense of superiority.

But that was then; this is now. Such a passive form of

patriotism, one that almost dare not speak its name for fear of frightening the horses, surely can't cut it in the modern world. Britain is now living with a set of circumstances and problems which are very much of this time, and many of which it has not faced before. Far from dying out in our supposedly globalised, international village of a world, regional and ethnic identities have, if anything, intensified. Lines are being redrawn. Religion is once again on the march – a remarkable fact that is simply not appreciated in Britain, which tends to assume that the decline in its own church-going is characteristic of the world in general. It is not. People are moving throughout the world in massive numbers, but the journeys tend to be one way: Westward, from poor to rich. The phenomenon of the internet, we were told by enthusiasts, would break down traditional geographical and national identities, and lead people to associate along completely new lines. There is no evidence that this has happened in any meaningful sense.

Perhaps a different approach when it comes to maintaining and expressing our own sense of identity is now required. As we saw in the last chapter, the ideas and orthodoxies that have held sway in Britain for the past half-century are gradually losing their grip. Hopefully the anti-nation, anti-patriotic, self-hating instincts which have wrought such damage are amongst them. We should take the opportunity to build on this.

Should we 'do' flags?

Despite being quite comfortable with the Union flag, there is still amongst many in Britain a sense that perhaps the Americans overdo things when it comes to their own star-spangled banner. On their numerous holidays to the US, many Brits find themselves being actually quite moved by the sheer number of ordinary houses, of all sizes and income brackets, which display the flag, sincerely and proudly. It stands in the school class room, flies from the city hall and is unfurled over shop entrances.

But it's something which many people would find difficult to imagine happening in Britain. Very occasionally, there is the chance here to be similarly moved: the rows of hundreds of Union flags which covered the length of Regent Street during the royal wedding left many quite awestruck, and was considered such a success it has been repeated for the jubilee. But this is one big exception that proves the rule. Politicians and commentators tend to laugh off the idea, when it is occasionally floated, that perhaps we could take a leaf out of America's book.

Well, perhaps we should, or if not the whole leaf then a smallish part of it. Perhaps we should, after all, start to 'do' flags. I am thinking here particularly of state schools, both primary and secondary, as the place where the presence of a Union flag would be most beneficial. It would indeed by the closest that children in many such schools would ever have come to it. Nobody is suggesting it be saluted as in the US, but just that – like a first-aid kit – every school should have one, and on prominent display.

And should there not too be a picture of the monarch? She is one of our most effective unifiers. Indeed, there is a strong case for suggesting that, far from retreating into irrelevance as its opponents claim, the monarchy's symbolic importance

as an institution which can and should bring an increasingly
fragmented society together is becoming of greater importance as the century goes on.

Reviving our powers of memory

We may not have done this kind of thing in the past. But
perhaps then we were safer in the knowledge that our values
and traditions were being transmitted, in the home, by families and by communities. In large sections of our society, this
is no longer the case. It might be regrettable to many that
something which should happen almost organically should
be, as it were, institutionalised in such a way. But we must
face facts. We can no longer rely on previous ways and methods. The process might have to be kick-started if it is to once
again become embedded.

If such a course were taken, one can envisage already the
kinds of protests that would come from the hostile teaching
and educational establishment. As most Secretaries of State for
Education find out sooner or later, this so-called 'progressive',
broadly left-wing establishment will fight tooth and nail to
preserve not just its rights but the methods and ideologies which
it has imposed on the educational system, and which have done
so much damage. Not for nothing do many see a fight with the
teaching unions as being as significant, in a cultural sense, as
Thatcher's confrontation with the miners in 1984.

Many teachers, prisoners as they are of old thinking
and discredited politics, are antipathetic to the whole idea
of preserving national identity through a proper telling of
Britain's national story. Instead they have seen education as

a means of changing society. Along with teaching the need for excellence, living with a Union Jack and a picture of the Queen nearby would be anathema to many of them. It would offend their beliefs, and their view of their role. If this is the case, then so be it. One of them will have to go.

The present Education Secretary, Michael Gove, is perhaps the first in a generation to truly appreciate the significance that the reform of education has in winning the culture wars, and is trying to grasp the nettle that so many have backed away from. It is hugely encouraging that a senior minister understands the premier role that schools should take in teaching and celebrating Britain's past. He has talked of the need to re-establish a proper chronological approach in history, and why children should once again learn about kings and queens. It was recently announced that he was to send every school a copy of the King James's Bible, to mark its recently celebrated 400th anniversary. This sort of gesture is to be applauded for its cultural symbolism. There needs to be many more like it. The establishment of the so-called Free Schools (which are not under local authority jurisdiction) is another step in the right direction if the hegemony of the educational establishment is to be broken for good.

There is another reason why a proper teaching of history is important to issues of identity and pride, which is not immediately obvious. A lack of the most basic historical knowledge can lead to a coarsened brand of patriotism which, lacking any depth or basis in real knowledge, is simultaneously sentimental and aggressive. It can play itself out on such occasions as sporting events, and admits to nothing special about itself, because nothing special is known; it becomes simply a case of us against them. Knowing what is remarkable and unique about your country actually prevents the boorishness which *Guardian*-readers in particular so often fear in any display of national identity.

Making clear what is unacceptable

Many of those same schools are now home to hundreds of different languages. It is now broadly accepted that newcomers, far from being encouraged to retain their language and culture completely intact, should learn English if they have any hope of integrating (a view which, as we have seen, was once considered racist). And if the children in these schools are to genuinely feel part of British society, they also need to have a strong idea of what they are meant to be integrating into. The fact that those charged with imparting British culture have either lost confidence in it, or actively think it shouldn't be passed on, has been a terrible barrier to this happening.

But the onus is also on us to make it clear what is and what is not acceptable in British culture. We looked earlier at the premise behind multiculturalism, and the way in which the continual emphasis on retaining individual cultures at the expense of integration had led to separation and fragmentation, with different groups living side by side but increasingly having little to do with each other. In this context, it is no longer beyond the pale to hold that multiculturalism has been a big mistake.

But the cultural relativism which accompanied it, and

which held that no judgement could or should be made about any minority culture, regardless of where it stood in relation to the values and beliefs of Britain as the host country, also resulted in an atmosphere where criticism was simply not allowed. This still largely pertains today.

The contradictions in this approach are becoming increasingly clear. Such relativism has posed liberal multiculturalists in particular with serious problems. They will hear no criticism of ethnic or religious minorities, whom they basically see as victims, and yet some of the beliefs and practices of those minorities conflict directly with their own values – and indeed with the values of wider British society.

So for example, the treatment meted out to some Muslim women by their own communities, including the practices of so-called 'honour killings' and female genital mutilation, still pass under the radar in Britain. There is virtually no criticism forthcoming from feminists, the very people who, one would think, should do everything they can to highlight such issues. The inaction on this, as on so many other issues, is the result of an almost pathological fear amongst such people of being called racist. Widespread homophobia, anti-semitism, the treatment of women as second-class citizens – all this has to be ignored if the multicultural narrative is to be upheld.

The Left in particular put themselves through intellectual somersaults in order to square the circle, and then finding they can't, simply pretend there is no problem. If, to take a hypothetical example, there were a case where the parents of a class of Muslim children took exception to an openly gay man teaching their children, there should be no question which side *The Guardian* should support. However, in the current atmosphere of trimming and obfuscation, that is far from guaranteed.

Once in a while a case comes along which is so ghastly it cannot be ignored. Light is thrown on it for a while, and then once again everybody backs away. In 2010 a black teenager named Kristy Bamu was horribly tortured and then murdered by a Congolese couple in Newham, London, who, obsessed by a belief in a form of witchcraft called *kindoki*, thought the boy was possessed by evil spirits. Belief in *kindoki* is widespread in the Congo, and it has become clear that this is far from being an isolated case in Britain. The extreme tentativeness which surrounds the treatment of literally life-and-death cases such as this one and the tragic killing in 2000 of Victoria Climbié, is the result of a seriously skewed sense of hypersensitivity to the practices of other cultures.

Not only should it be stated loud and clear that such practices (which, while hiding under the cloak of religion, are mostly purely cultural ones) are an affront to all notions of decency and basic morality. It should be made clear from the highest points in our society that they are utterly incompatible with our values, and will in no circumstances be tolerated. They should be eradicated completely.

Minding our manners

Britain was once famed for its courtesy and social orderliness, and in turn was proud of the reputation. Much of the low-level anti-social behaviour which makes our lives just that bit more stressful, and which we looked at earlier, derives from a breakdown in the transmission of simple communal values. If you do not socialise children at the most basic level, if you do not teach them to even acknowledge the presence of others, much less show them respect, then eventually you end up with the kind of situation which many of us endure on a daily basis. The boorish, the selfish and the yobbish are in charge of many public places, and we find ourselves working around them.

It might go completely against the grain of a society that has always cherished liberty, but perhaps to stop the rot from going further, we will have to have a more regulatory approach. For example, I described earlier the breakdown in queuing in many urban areas. In order to revive it, perhaps we should introduce a ticketing system of the type we're all used to using at the supermarket delicatessen counter. People appear to have no trouble with it in those circumstances; they abide by it and don't feel that they're being treated like children. Perhaps the time has come to institute such a system at our city bus stops.

This will certainly strike some as laughably small-fry. But the truth is a much broader social revival can come from just such tiny adjustments. One only has to look at the 'broken windows' principle which was behind New York's stunningly successful policy of zero tolerance towards crime. You start from the ground up, taking care of the little things and increasingly the big things, if not taking care of themselves, certainly start to diminish. Likewise, a system of fines could be introduced to help promote the sort of behaviour on public transport (which does not include spitting and using seats as footrests) which, up until recently, we could have assumed would come naturally to most of us.

If you cannot rely on parents passing on such traditions and values, as is the case in many areas, then perhaps the time has come for people to be refamiliarised with them in other ways. This more formalised approach needn't even be permanent, but could be enforced only for as long as it took to get people back into the habit of treating their fellow citizens with proper fairness and consideration.

Offended? Tough

Freedom of Speech is one of the most basic of British values. However, the throwaway line 'it's a free country', which was once often heard, increasingly feels as if it has, in fact, been thrown away.

Much of the reason for this has to do with a culture of offence which has taken hold, and which goes against the robust traditions of public argument and intellectual cut and thrust which Britain has always enjoyed. We have become tentative and sheepish in a way which Europeans often find remarkable and indeed depressing. Political correctness has taken root far more firmly here than in most Western countries, save perhaps the USA (where it originated). Such is the oppressiveness of the atmosphere now, it is probably likely that many people quite genuinely believe that they have a legal right not to be offended.

No such right exists, and neither should it. Right now, our news is regularly peppered with stories about perceived offence given or taken, stories which then become mini-controversies played out on radio phone-ins and news-paper columns. It is exasperating, and morale sapping, as it always tends to be when walking on egg shells. And it has a considerable effect on the shape and drift of British public life.

We looked at the arts earlier on, as the arch-practitioners of political correctness. With one or two honourable exceptions, the self-appointed holders of the beacon of free speech have in fact become arch self-censors, careful not to give offence to this or that group or religion. Some of these, of course, remain fair game, but they tend to be the groups who will not answer back or at least pose no real danger, and are accustomed to be being used as target practice – Christians, for example. Monty Python's *The Life of Brian* might have upset some people when it was released over thirty years ago, but it could be made in the knowledge that no buildings would be razed to the ground, no people killed. Decades later, *Jerry Springer: The Opera*, with its portrayal of Jesus in a nappy, could still run in the West End and be broadcast by the BBC. But the chances of there being a *Life of Iqbal* are virtually nil.

There is sometimes little basis to the fear of giving offence. This has turned out to be the case in those instances, much beloved by the tabloids, where overprotective, nervy local authorities have attempted to ban or change various local traditions or customs for fear of 'excluding' or 'offending' this or that group, who, it often transpires, then profess them-selves blithely unconcerned. But the lack of offence taken is ignored, so entrenched has the fear of giving it become.

This has also affected the strong tradition of British satire, which is currently at a low ebb. Church and monarchy, the law and the establishment – all these institutions have been mocked to death over the years to the point where no self-respecting, aspiring satirist could seriously consider taking them on again. But is there not still a wealth of material out there? Could not the absurdities of political correctness alone fill a whole TV series? Or how about the various mantras of multiculturalism? Or the argument over the wearing of the burqa? Are such topics not ripe for the satirist's ruthless dissection? Of course they are. But they remain untouched. Amazing as it may seem, a fear of the very reaction it is actually meant to provoke has finally silenced satire. Instead, we are left with 'edgy' comedians who somehow equate mocking the mentally disabled or the Queen's genitalia with cutting-edge transgression.

The whining over offence, and the huge emphasis put on the need to publicly apologise for real or imagined slights, is a sign of an infantilised society, one which needs to be constantly stroked and placated. We must start treating each other, whether individual or group, as adults again.

Time to give a lead?

And finally, there is a role to be played by our politicians – our discredited, disrespected and demoralised politicians.

We are living in the midst of a recession at the moment, one which has come on the tail of a financial crisis the like of which had not been seen for decades. Britain has weathered many a recession in the past, and although we are told that this is like no other, we will, without wishing to be complacent, doubtless weather this one too. Capitalism however, is talked of as being in crisis, as needing 'reform' (whatever that might mean) and as having somehow 'failed' us.

But the fact is that broadly speaking, the economic war, by which I mean the arguments over the very basis on which our society should be run, really took place some decades ago. It was then that the fierce battle over whether the future was a socialist or a capitalist one was fought. And despite the events of the past few years, capitalism's triumph in that war has not really been dimmed by the cries we might hear now about the dysfunction of its banking system, or its supposed corruption by a casino mentality (both of which may or may not be true). Rather, the fact that nobody seriously suggests an alternative along socialistic lines is proof that the fundamentals of our economic system are settled.

But our culture, on the other hand, is beset by huge and pressing questions. On these fundamental issues, there is barely a word to be heard from our political class.

I mentioned earlier how President Sarkozy had made a speech in which he implored his country to throw off the yoke of cultural self-hatred that was the legacy of the so-called 'Sixty-Eighters'. It was invigorating then to hear a politician acknowledge the importance to his country of a cultural phenomenon that wasn't immediately an economic one; he understood the extent of the influence that a set of ideas could have, and paid his audience the compliment of assuming they understood too.

Could not our own senior politicians take a lead from the French (for once) and address such broader issues? Why in Britain do they have to be left to media commentators and newspaper columnists? Could we not hear David Cameron address the culture of debilitating self-criticism that has so blighted Britain, and explain why it has become so entrenched? Could not a senior minister make a speech which talks about British identity in a way which is devoid of the obvious cynicism which hedged Gordon Brown's, and which unequivocally celebrates it? Could we not have leaders who don't feel obliged to issue diplomatic apologies to other nations on our behalf? Leaders who speak of the importance of patriotism, instead of trying to douse it, or nervously back away from it?

It's no longer enough for our politicians to claim that that's just not their style, that they don't 'do' this kind of cultural thing. They might like to try. And who knows, British people might start listening to them again.

CHAPTER NINE

BEING BRITISH:
WHAT'S RIGHT WITH IT

I started this book with an anecdote about an overheard conversation between two assistants in a London bookshop. What had the British ever given the world, asked one with a smirk, before dismissively answering his own question: concentration camps. As I have described, I said nothing, but quietly festered (now, how British is that!). If I'd had the Internet to hand, I could have replied that actually, concentration camps appear to have been an eighteenth-century Polish invention. But no matter, such an answer would have been dancing to their negative tune anyway.

We'll return to my bookshop friends a bit later, but it's worth pondering at this point whether being patriotic, if you define that as loving the country you're from, automatically includes pride in the international impact it has had – 'what it has given the world'. I think that clearly it does not. A love for your country and its institutions might well lead

logically to a great appreciation of its international achievements, but one can still exist without the other. There are
many of younger generations now in Britain who might feel
a sense of national identity while having no real notion of, for
example, the British Empire. And people can still feel a great
attachment to their country even if it is one which has tended
to plough a lonely furrow, detached from the global stage. I'm
sure that the Swiss have a great fondness for Switzerland.

A patriotic feeling can be, for want of a better descrip-
tion, completely domestic. Sometimes, an affection which
one could call vaguely patriotic can arise from such seemingly banal things as a great familiarity with, and liking for, a
certain type of landscape. It can be a fondness for a particular
way of looking at the world. It can come from a sense of
shared humour, or a liking for the way in which your fellow
country men and women express themselves to each other.

I recall a journalist describing this feeling as she watched
the television show *Britain's Got Talent*, which always includes
a succession of eccentric no-hopers along with the occasional
talented discovery. It might seem an odd way to experience a
funny little patriotic twinge, but I know what she meant. I've
sometimes had this sensation when listening to conversations
between groups of friends in my local pub. Their quips and
teasing, and reactions to each other as they make plans, makes
me feel a certain sort of warmth towards them, even though
they are complete strangers. It doesn't make me want to go
and hang up bunting – it's much more subtle and low-key
than that. It's simply that you find yourself having a fondness
for the people around you.

Is this not another way of defining what we mean when we talk about a sense of identity – when you literally identify with those around you? Is this not then part of what we call *national* identity? We are talking after all about familiarity, about the sense that you will have some things in common, that there will be shared cultural or historical references. Location, while providing a strong link between people, is not usually enough on its own.

Such subliminal things are what we miss, I think, when we talk of being homesick. Fleeing the irony-thick atmosphere of London in the late 1990s, I went to live in Los Angeles, where I stayed for five years. That was me done with England, I thought. I had always had – and still do – a huge fondness for America, and like many British people my gaze has always tended towards the Atlantic rather than the English Channel (diehards would claim that America itself was one of the biggest things Britain gave the world). The sheer weight of the past can be like a monkey on the back of the Europeans, and Americans sometimes fail to understand that it is the resolute sense of the here and now in their country which attracts us in the first place. They still tend to direct us towards places like San Francisco, with its more 'European' (for which read 'refined') sensibility. That is not, however, what we tend to go there for.

But after five years of the here and now, I had certainly started to get regular flickers of longing for the there and then, for the old country, which I tended to repress. But in the end they proved irresistible. It was small things: a longing to feel moist air and to wear my overcoat; increasing trips to the international news-stands for British papers; a surprising level of interest in the ongoing preparations for the Queen Mother's funeral; a longing not to have to explain a joke; a desire to see old, chipped paint that wasn't just another stylistic effect.

It's a cliché but nevertheless true that sometimes you have to lose something before you realise its value. The same goes for countries. But that does not mean that you then take them back uncritically. Being proud of your country does not require that you should lose your sense of judgement or discrimination; you do not have to love everything about it. For example I certainly found myself at odds with the resolutely downwardly aspirational tone of much of British life in the first years of the new century, when there appeared to be the desire to wallow in crudity. You can make as many references as you like to Hogarth and his depictions of Gin Lane, but nothing will make the sight of Saturday night town-centre binge drinking anything less than an ugly one. But equally to take from this the view, as some have done, that such behaviour represents the very essence of British culture is completely mistaken and unfair, like judging a pupil's overall ability on his worst set of marks. And neither should it be used as yet another excuse to beat ourselves up.

The state of Britain in the years immediately after my return – the malaise, the problems and the changes which I have outlined in the preceding pages – originally caused me to despair. But then, perhaps taking a leaf from the book of my American experiences, I thought you can either stand in the kitchen and moan or you can join the party. Perhaps it's always better if people try to do something. In my case, it has been writing this book.

What we have

I hope, if you have read this far, and even find yourself agreeing with my analysis, that you are not one of those who feel like giving up on Britain. It's more than likely that, if the survey we looked at earlier is to be believed, you are one of the 79 per cent who consider themselves proud to be British. So you should take heart from the fact that the last thing you are is alone, although it must seem like it sometimes. That's hardly surprising when you consider the scale of the problems that Britain has experienced, the sense that it has been battered from all sides and the ingrained self-loathing amongst those who shape its culture.

Whether or not you also agree with the few suggestions I have put forward for enhancing a cohesive sense of identity and boosting our sense of Britishness, I hope the cultural malaise we have faced has not blinded you to what is right about being British.

For the fact is that this is a truly remarkable country. I am not just talking here about its geography or political stability. It is fair to say that there is hardly a single part of our every-day lives that has not in some way been affected or shaped by British method, inventiveness or industrial innovation. As the first country to industrialise, Britain essentially created the modern age. From the magnifying glass down to the World Wide Web, its inventors have been pioneers without equal. Its contribution to science is equally unique – indeed it invented science in the modern sense.

How men see themselves has been hugely influenced by this country's literature. It essentially created the modern novel. Its greatest writer, Shakespeare, is also the world's greatest writer. Its political development has been a testament to the power of reform over bloody revolution.

The point has been made before but can be made again: the impact that this country has had on the world is extraordinary. This is especially so given its size. America might be the world's superpower but it has a hell of a lot of land and people to draw on; Britain could comfortably fit into California with room to spare. Historians have tried to explain this hugely disproportionate influence, sometimes in terms of lucky timing, sometimes even in terms of favourable climate conditions (other countries wouldn't be so self-effacing). But however it came to pass, these small islands ended up shaping the world in which we now live.

The British Empire might have been regarded by many in the period we have covered in this book as a source of shame – although thankfully some balance is now being restored to the picture. The legacies it left in individual countries were by no means all negative ones. But even when just seen as a feat of administrative, commercial and military power, the Empire was a quite extraordinary achievement. It might have started as something of an accident, but at its height, it covered nearly a quarter of the world's land surface and over 450 million of its people. After the war, it was dismantled, too, with remarkable speed and little resistance on the part of the British. Whereas my parents' generation was perhaps the last to grow up with a genuine sense of the country's imperial power, for those of us born in the 1950s and 1960s, the Empire simply meant fleeting TV images of flags being lowered in some far-flung place in the presence of a minor royal in white uniform.

I think it would be fair to say that a hankering after a departed imperial past does not play much part in most people's sense of national pride now. The patriotism they might feel is couched more at home than in the outward bound: the defence of Britain in 1940 by 'the few' is vastly more potent as a national memory today than, say, the British Raj. But this is not to say that they would rather not talk about the Empire, or have consciously rejected it in some way. Rather, they see it as an episode in the country's history, an extraordinary one perhaps, but an episode nonetheless, alongside Magna Carta, the defeat of the Spanish Armada and Nelson's victory at Trafalgar. And it is that history, with its catalogue of astonishing world-class achievements, which is at the basis of their sense of pride. It certainly is of mine.

As we said earlier on, identifying with your country to the extent that you love it can be based on a liking for its ways, its humour, or the fact that you feel, quite simply, that it is, in a way which is hard to define, special; that for all its faults, it is the best place in which to live. That such a feeling still exists in Britain is all the more remarkable when one considers the onslaught it has endured over the past half a century, and which we have looked at in this book. A sense of national identity, and a pride in that identity, might once have been reflected by and in those who led Britain from the top. But now, such a feeling is held *in spite of* those who, in all their different forms and incarnations, presume to lead us, and *in the face of* those who have power over our cultural and political fate.

All the more reason, then, not to rely on politicians, nor just to wait for pollsters to ask us questions, but to speak up more often. You might be familiar with a now classic scene from Monty Python's *Life of Brian*, in which John Cleese, surrounded by his followers in the People's Popular Front of Judea (or is it the Judea People's Popular Front?) asks angrily 'What have the Romans ever done for us?' One by one the motley crew volunteer various achievements, leaving Cleese eventually exasperated and defeated.

I'm reminded of that scene when I think of my two book-shop assistants. So by way of a conclusion, and to help you out if ever you find yourself in a similar situation and lost for words, I've written here fifty handy suggestions – from the groundbreaking to the quirky – to that same question, 'What have the British ever given the world?'

I will certainly be taking a leaf out of my own book from now on. The list, by the way, is in no particular order, and is by no means exhaustive. But it's a start.

The industrial revolution

Taking place from the mid-eighteenth to the mid-nineteenth centuries, the transformation wrought by the mechanisation of all aspects of manufacturing and agriculture essentially ushered in the modern age. What began in Britain, as a result of British ingenuity, inventiveness and enterprise, eventually spread throughout the rest of the globe, changing the way life was lived forever.

Parliamentary democracy

As the Mother of Parliaments, Britain has been the biggest exporter of a system of government which developed over centuries through incremental reform, constant revision, tradition and one or two moments of serious conflict. Much emulated throughout the world, the British model remains for many the best guard against the corruption which besets so many other systems – a belief that remains largely intact despite the dishonour brought upon Westminster itself by the petty deceptions of the current generation of parliamentarians.

William Shakespeare

Nearly 400 years after this death, the position of Shakespeare (1564–1616) as the benchmark by which all literature is judged is unassailable. Translated and performed in countless languages, his plays and poetry remain the backbone to all studies of literature and drama. Still a remarkably enigmatic figure, his identity is frequently the object of investigation, but his achievement is never in doubt; there is never a moment when his plays are not being performed somewhere. Our everyday speech is, unbeknown to most of us, peppered with words and phrases introduced into the language by him.

The concept of evolution, as developed by Charles Darwin

One of the most important books ever written, Darwin's

On the Origin of Species (1859) proposed the scientific theory that evolution was the result of a process of natural selection. Popularly accepted remarkably quickly given its revolutionary nature, it is impossible to overstate the full extent of its remarkable global influence, although in our time the teaching of evolution is banned in some Muslim countries. On his death Darwin (1809–1882) was given a full ceremonial funeral in Westminster Abbey; in 2002 he was voted one of the top ten Greatest Britons of all time.

The concept and laws of gravity, as discovered by Sir Isaac Newton

Considered to be the greatest scientist who ever lived, Newton (1642–1727), wrote *Philosophiæ Naturalis Principia Mathematica* (1687), which described universal gravitation, and is regarded as the most important scientific book in human history. Also a mathematician, philosopher and astronomer, Newton famously (and modestly) described himself as having just stood 'on the shoulders of giants', but the English poet Pope was nearer to the mark when he wrote: 'Nature and nature's laws lay hid by night; God said "Let Newton be" and all was light.'

The World Wide Web, as invented by Sir Tim Berners-Lee

Computer scientist Berners-Lee (born 1955) is famous not just for this world-altering invention, but also for the fact that he left his idea deliberately unpatented and therefore free (considering his achievement, his name is still less well known than some eighteenth-century inventors). The first website was built at CERN in France in 1991. In 1999 Berners-Lee was named by *Time* magazine one of the 100 most important people of the twentieth century.

Common Law

An ancient system of law which is based on precedent, or the decisions of past cases, Common Law was first codified into a proper country-wide system in England by Henry II in the mid-twelfth century. Its strength traditionally lies in its flexibility and ability to evolve with changing times and mores. It now forms the basis of the legal systems in the United States, Canada, Australia, South Africa and Zimbabwe and many other countries which were once British colonies.

English, the global language

Now perhaps the first truly global method of communication (to the eternal chagrin of the French), English is the language of business, communications and diplomacy throughout the world – not to mention entertainment. A billion people speak it. Its current status as the world's lingua franca developed from its use within the British Empire and the subsequent rise of the USA as a global superpower. The *Oxford English Dictionary* lists over 250,000 words, which include words and phrases from countless other languages.

The King James Bible

The 400th anniversary in 2011 of this, perhaps the most influential single book in the English language, was marked by many events and celebrations. It has been described as the only great work of art to be created by a committee. Fifty-four scholars worked for seven years on the new translation of the Bible at the behest of James I. 'The scholars who produced this masterpiece are mostly unknown and unremembered,' said Churchill. 'But they forged an enduring link, literary and religious, between the English-speaking people of the world.'

Penicillin, as discovered by Alexander Fleming

Fleming (1881–1955), a Scottish biologist, won the Nobel Prize for his world-changing discovery; at the end of the last millennium *Time* magazine named him one of the most important people of the twentieth century. Astonishingly, there was a gap of twelve years between the discovery and its first use, in 1941. Penicillin would go on to treat effectively countless bacterial infections and hitherto fatal diseases such as tuberculosis and syphilis.

The scientific method, as developed by Francis Bacon

Bacon (1561–1626) has been called the creator of empiricism, and his work has been credited with laying the foundations by which scientific enquiry was henceforth carried out. Also a philosopher, he laid out the moral and practical grounds for the industrialisation which followed in the eighteenth century. His nineteenth-century biographer William Hepworth Dixon summarised Bacon's immense achievements and influence thus:

Every man who rides in a train, who sends a telegram, who follows a steam plough, who sits in an easy chair, who crosses the channel or Atlantic, who eats a good dinner, who enjoys a beautiful garden, or undergoes a painless operation, owes him something.

Anaesthetic in the use of surgery, as pioneered by Joseph Lister

Lister (1827–1912) was the first surgeon to use anaesthesia and antisepsis and in doing so transformed the standards of safety in medical procedures. He invented the sinus forceps and probe-pointed scissors still used today. The popular mouthwash Listerine was named in his honour when it first appeared in the nineteenth century.

Charlie Chaplin

The son of south London music hall entertainers, Charlie Chaplin (1889–1977) went on to become, in his incarnation as the little tramp, one of the few instantly recognisable cultural icons of the twentieth century. His winsome persona endeared him to audiences and he went on to achieve a kind of fame which had not really existed before – that of the global entertainer. The character he created is still known now to generations who have never seen a silent film.

An Inquiry into the Nature and Causes of The Wealth of Nations by Adam Smith.

A Scottish economist and philosopher, Smith (bap. 1723–1790) published *The Wealth of Nations* in 1776. It is regarded as one of the most important and influential treatises on economics ever published, and, in promoting the idea of individual enterprise as the key to economic prosperity, is to this day venerated especially by those with a belief in the virtues of free market capitalism. The former Chairman of the US Federal Reserve, Alan Greenspan, described *The Wealth of Nations* as 'one of the great achievements in human intellectual history'.

The art of J. M. W. Turner

Hugely prolific in both oils and watercolour, Joseph Mallord William Turner (1775–1851) is considered the greatest British artist of Romantic landscapes. His work was to prove of huge and lasting international influence. His 1839 picture *The Fighting Temeraire* was voted the greatest British painting of all time in a public poll in 2005. The famous annual Turner Prize was named after him, although he should not be held responsible for this.

Power looms, as invented by Edmund Cartwright

A clergyman from Nottinghamshire, Cartwright (1743–1823) was to revolutionise mechanical weaving in the years which followed the patenting of his power loom in 1785. Many improvements followed, and by 1850 there were a quarter of a million of the machines operating in Britain.

Abolition of the slave trade

The Slave Trade Act of 1807 abolished slavery, the end result of a largely religiously motivated movement which had begun in the 1770s and which by the time the Act was passed had been led for some time by the Yorkshireman Sir William Wilberforce. Other countries such as France, Sweden and Spain followed suit in the years directly after. The British Navy used its then incomparable might to enforce abolition across the globe, and within the next half a century 150,000 slaves were freed.

Mass production of steel, as developed by Henry Bessemer
An English engineer and prolific inventor, Bessemer (1813–1898) developed a method for the much cheaper production of steel, which could then be used on an industrial scale.

Football, rugby, cricket, golf – virtually all organised sport
Although people have played games since time immemorial, for all practical purposes, organised, modern sport in most of its various guises originated in Britain. It was here that its rules were codified and where its first associations – the MCC, the Football Association – were set up. It matters not that the British performance in all the numerous fields of play is now extremely variable, for if it is indeed the playing of the game that truly matters, then organised sport is one of Britain's great altruistic gestures to the world. Spread far and wide as an offshoot of the Empire, these games in their different ways still display aspects of the British social character, but are now universal and as such owned by the world. The hope, however, that 'football's coming home' springs eternal in the breasts of millions of British fans.

The Lord of the Rings by J. R. R. Tolkien

Tolkien (1892–1973), an Oxford professor, published *The Hobbit* in 1937 and then followed it with this, his epic three-part fantasy, in the 1950s. Hundreds of millions of copies have been sold worldwide and the meanings and themes of each pored over and analysed. The film adaptation by director Peter Jackson was phenomenally successful, both financially and critically: the final instalment, *The Return of the King*, won eleven Academy Awards.

The human circulatory system, as discovered by William Harvey

The Kent-born Harvey (1578–1657) was the first person to describe in detail the method by which the heart pumped blood around the system. A doctor at London's famous Bart's Hospital, he published his famous work, *de Motu Cordis*, in 1628. He was physician to both James I and Charles I.

James Bond, as created by Ian Fleming

Bond, or 007 as he is known, is the fictional British Secret Service agent who first appeared in 1953 in Fleming's *Casino Royale*. First portrayed on screen by Sean Connery in *Dr No* in 1962, he became a global icon of a certain sort of Britishness, one born of the Cold War and Macmillan era. In the decades and five further actors since, the Bond series has made nearly $5 billion, although for some of that time the character slipped into parody. As the latest incumbent, Daniel Craig is generally considered to have restored Bond's credibility. His introductory line 'Bond ... James Bond' is known even to those who've never read a book or seen a film.

The jet engine, as invented by Sir Frank Whittle

Initially receiving remarkably little official encouragement or support, Whittle (1907–1996), an RAF engineer, persevered with the groundbreaking work that would eventually lead to the invention of the turbojet engine, one of most important achievements of the twentieth century. Early stresses took a considerable toll on his health, but in the post-war years he received universal recognition. Air travel of the kind the world takes for granted today simply would not have happened without him.

Peter Pan, as created by J. M. Barrie

The boy who refused to grow up first appeared in 1902, and since then has become a worldwide star of stage, screen and television, even giving his name to a psychological complex. Barrie's creation, who lives with his gang of Lost Boys in Neverland, is not an altogether sympathetic character, but his cocky irresponsibility continues to enthral children of all ages across the world as he enters his second century.

Brit Art

Love them or hate them (and much of the British press hates them) artists like Damien Hirst and Tracey Emin, who were at the forefront of the sudden explosion in British art in the 1990s, have pushed the output of our contemporary culture into the global spotlight.

The smallpox vaccination, as discovered by Edward Jenner

Known now as the father of immunology, Jenner (1749–1823), a doctor and scientist, was widely ridiculed after famously inoculating 8-year-old James Phipps with cow pus. But the experiment proved the correctness of his hypothesis, and resulted thereafter in the saving of countless lives from the then deadly killer smallpox.

The steam engine

Thomas Newcomen (bap. 1664–1729), an ironmonger, invented the first practical steam engine, which was named after him. But it was hugely improved later in the eighteenth century by the Scottish inventor and engineer James Watt (1736–1819), and became quite literally the engine which drove the industrial revolution in Britain and henceforth the world. The unit of power, the watt, is named after him.

Paradise Lost by John Milton

One of the greatest works of English literature, Milton's epic poem from 1667 about the fall of man has continued to have a profound cultural resonance, whether it be in influencing the work of William Blake, or informing popular Hollywood films such as *Seven* and *The Devil's Advocate*.

The 'CAT' scanner, as invented by Sir Godfrey N. Houndsfield

This vital piece of modern medical machinery was invented by the little known engineer Houndsfield (1919–2004) who, along with his collaborator Allan Mcleod Cormack, was awarded the Nobel Prize for his efforts. Houndsfield, who did not go to university and was largely self-taught, originally developed it simply as a way of gaining a three-dimensional image of the inside of a living organism.

Harry Potter, as created by J. K. Rowling

Over fifteen years the seven Harry Potter books have together sold over 400 million copies worldwide, and the boy wizard now easily stands alongside those other fictional creations like Peter Pan and Sherlock Holmes as being part of global culture. Joanne Rowling's own remarkable rags-to-riches story is known to everyone and her achievement in getting children to read again (as well as many of their parents) cannot be overstated. The cinema adaptations have been equally phenomenally successful, creating a virtually separate film industry on their own.

The structure of DNA, as discovered by Francis Crick and James Watson

In 1953 Crick, along with his American collaborator Watson, made one of the twentieth century's most important – if not *the* most important – scientific breakthroughs: the establishment of the double helix structure of the DNA molecule within the human cell. Apparently Crick visited the local pub that same day and announced, 'We have found the secret of life.' They were awarded the Nobel Prize in 1962.

The hovercraft, as invented by Sir Christopher Cockerell

As with other inventors, Cockerell (1910–1999) was often

starved of cash from official sources when attempting to put ideas, which would later be regarded as revolutionary, into practice. Starting out with tin cans and an air blower to develop his notion of movement on a cushion of air, he eventually produced a working model in 1955. The hovercraft went on to become one of the emblems of post-war technological progress.

Sherlock Holmes, as created by Sir Arthur Conan Doyle

So familiar across the world is the famous fictional detective that he is assumed by many who beat a path to his famous address at 221b Baker Street to have been a real person. Featuring in sixty stories written by Conan Doyle, he remains the most portrayed film character, including memorably Basil Rathbone (fourteen times). Benedict Cumberbatch successfully updated the character to modern times for television. Aficionados, however, consider the British actor Jeremy Brett to have been the definitive Holmes. The detective's worldwide appeal shows no signs of diminishing.

Frankenstein, as created by Mary Shelley

Shelley's gothic novel *Frankenstein, or The Modern Prometheus*, first appeared in 1818. The monster, sewn together by the eponymous scientist, long since outgrew the page and is now a universally known fictional character, made famous by countless films, although many still confuse the maker and his ghastly creation. As portrayed in the 1930s by the exotic-sounding Boris Karloff (who was in fact a British gent by the name of William Henry Pratt), the monster, with his flat head, bolted neck and lumbering walk, now belongs to global popular culture.

The world's first modern postal service

Methods of posting of one kind or another have been around for some time of course, but it was the reforms of Sir Rowland Hill (1795–1879), and his introduction of pre-paid postage of varying rates, which essentially created the modern mass postal service as the world now knows it.

British television

It might be that our real glory days are behind us here, but only a few decades ago British TV was routinely talked of as the best in the world. Whether it was the surreal humour of *Monty Python*, the slapstick of *Mr Bean* or the drama of *Brideshead Revisited* and *Upstairs Downstairs*, British programmes were exported across the globe and became popular viewing and henceforth highly influential in other countries. This remains true, even if the formats have changed: game and quiz shows which started here are now staples on TV channels throughout the world.

Miss Marple and Hercule Poirot, as created by Agatha Christie

These two fictional detectives from another, perhaps gentler age are alive and well and playing on a screen somewhere near you now. The perennially popular Dame Agatha (1890–1976) wrote over sixty detective novels, but it is Marple and Poirot who, thanks to continual film and television adaptations, are known throughout the world.

The Beatles

British pop and rock music has shown astonishing variety and innovation over the past five decades, but in terms of popularity alone the fabulous four from Liverpool still stand head and shoulders above their nearest rivals. John, Paul, George and Ringo broke up over forty years ago, but their music remains as significant – and as enjoyed – as ever. Their immense worldwide success in the 1960s was followed by a stream of British bands and entertainers who became some of the biggest names in contemporary music and entertainment – from the Rolling Stones, David Bowie and Elton John to the Spice Girls, Florence + the Machine and Adele.

The BBC

First formed in 1922 and then confirmed under a Royal Charter in 1927, the BBC remains perhaps the most famous broadcasting service in the world. It is certainly the largest, with over 20,000 staff. For almost the same length of time it has operated the BBC World Service (which started out as the BBC Empire Service), which still stretches across the globe, broadcasting in twenty-six languages as well as English. The standards of BBC journalism have been held in particularly high regard, with tens of millions tuning in to its news and programmes.

Sir Alfred Hitchcock

Hitchcock (1899–1980) has been called the most influential director of all time; certainly he is the greatest film-maker Britain has ever produced. Originally from London's East

End, his career spanned six decades, including periods spent in both Britain and Hollywood, and countless classics, from *Rebecca* and *Foreign Correspondent* to *Vertigo* and, of course, *Psycho*. His reputation as the master of suspense is almost too limiting, when one considers the extent of his influence on myriad film genres and directors since.

The music of Benjamin Britten

British classical music flourished in the twentieth century, and Britten (1913–1976) was at the very forefront. Through his operas, such as *Peter Grimes*, *Billy Budd* and *The Turn of the Screw*, his reputation become truly international and his work remains in the repertory. He founded the internationally prestigious Aldeburgh Festival, which takes place annually at Snape Maltings in Suffolk.

Sir Winston Churchill

Despite the occasional 'revisionist' attempts to lessen his standing, Churchill (1874–1965) remains revered today, not just in Britain – where he is virtually beyond criticism – but in Europe, the US and around the world. It is true to say that he is something 'we have given the world' because it was his leadership at a crucial point in the Second World War that kept Hitler at bay and in doing so prevented the world from slipping deeper into the abyss. And despite his name carrying with it the very essence of Britishness, there is something international about him as an individual, in that the sheer extent of his talents, wit and force of character are an inspiration to people everywhere.

The novels of Charles Dickens

The widespread celebrations of Dickens's bicentenary in 2012 were testament to his undiminished fame, and the special place he holds in the British imagination. However, the characters he created are known throughout the English-speaking world and beyond, thanks in large part to the countless cinema and television adaptations: Scrooge, Fagin, Mr Micawber and Oliver are familiar even to those who have never read the books. Modern writers regularly attempt to emulate the grand social sweep of Dickens's panoramic novels; most of them fail.

The cat's eye, as invented by Percy Shaw

Shaw (1890–1976) was the Yorkshire-born inventor who came up with the simple idea of reflecting road studs. There are a number of different stories as to how he got the idea, the most famous being that it came to him when he saw his headlamps reflected in the eyes of a cat when driving one night. Many a fractious child on a long car journey has been kept occupied by that story.

Electromagnetism, as developed by Michael Faraday

Faraday's contribution to the study of electromagnetism and electrochemistry was immense: he discovered electro-magnetic induction, the basic principle behind the electric transformer and generator. For such an influential and important figure, Faraday (1791–1867) was, astonishingly, largely self-taught.

The music of Edward Elgar

The more popularly known music of Elgar (1857–1934), such as his *Pomp & Circumstance* marches, was for many years held to be too imperialistic for modern tastes and so his overall output also suffered from critical neglect and disparagement. This has changed in more recent times, and his position as one of Britain's greatest composers has now been affirmed. His work, including the *Enigma Variations*, the cello concerto and *The Dream of Gerontius*, features firmly in the international classical repertory.

Railways

The *Locomotion*, a steam locomotive, was built by the inventor and engineer George Stephenson and in 1825 was used on the famous Stockton and Darlington Railway, the first public steam railway in the world. Four years later, Stephenson produced the famous *Rocket*. Railways grew exponentially and by the middle of that century, there were over 7,000 miles of them throughout the country. Where Britain led, the rest of the world followed.

1984 by George Orwell

Published in 1948, the title of this classic novel has entered the language worldwide as a byword for authoritarian dystopia, as indeed has the adjective 'Orwellian', again usually to denote the uses and abuses of power by regimes with tyrannical intent. Orwell, also the author of the equally important political parable *Animal Farm*, died two years later, full of foreboding for the future. Interestingly, although a quarter of a century has passed since the title date, the fear of 'Big Brother', the Ministry of Truth and the threat of a future as a 'boot stamping on a human face forever' have lost none of their urgency or global relevance

Winnie-the-Pooh, as created by A. A. Milne

The 'Bear of Very Little Brain' featured as the main character in just two children's books by the early twentieth-century British children's author (*Winnie the Pooh* and *The House at Pooh Corner*), but his worldwide fame was such that Walt Disney considered him as valid a subject for a cartoon adaptation as Cinderella or Sleeping Beauty. A Latin version, *Winnie ille Pu*, became a *New York Times* bestseller in 1958.

Viagra

British scientists have been credited with developing the sexual wonder drug of the modern age, although initially it seems to have been a rather accidental discovery: the drug was meant to treat heart problems, but produced this rather interesting side effect...

So, that's fifty things Britain has given the world. All lists tend to be idiosyncratic but I hope that there's something for everybody on it. I would add that I have left out those achievements where there was even a sliver of doubt or controversy, or where the credit could in some way be spread further afield than these shores. For example, John Logie

Baird was the first man to give a practical demonstration of working television (in central London in 1926) and could justly claim to have invented it, but his system lost out a decade later in favour of Marconi's in the US. If you feel that I'm being too pedantic here, too backward in coming forward in blowing Britain's trumpet, then please do write and let me know.

I hope too that some of the names, inventions and ideas on the list come as a surprise to some people, and that it starts discussion amongst family and friends. Doubtless, as with all lists, some will be outraged at what I have omitted. Why Churchill, for example, and no Nelson? Why Dickens and not Jane Austen? To this I would reply that these fifty had and continue to have significant worldwide importance. Churchill's role was a global one in the way that Nelson's perhaps wasn't. Dickens's individual characters are familiar throughout the world in the way that Austen's aren't.

None of which is to say that we shouldn't be intensely proud of the achievements of either Nelson or Austen. Indeed, if we change the emphasis to concern ourselves more simply with great figures from our history – people we admire regardless of the worldwide impact they might have had – a new list emerges, which again could go on and on. Perhaps, inspired by this book, you'd like to start compiling one.

I will start you off: Wellington, Sir Francis Drake, Noël Coward, Evelyn Waugh, Isambard Kingdom Brunel, Scott of the Antarctic, Florence Nightingale, Laurence Olivier, Elizabeth I, Chaucer, Captain Cook, Emmeline Pankhurst, Douglas Bader, David Livingstone...